Double Dads One Teen

A Queer Family's Trailblazing Life in the USA and Taiwan

Stuart F. Chen-Hayes, Ph.D.

Lehman College of the City University of New York

ISBN 978-1-64504-013-2 (Hardback)
ISBN 978-1-64504-012-5 (Paperback)
ISBN 978-1-64504-014-9 (E-Book)

Printed on acid-free paper

© DIO Press Inc, New York
https://www.diopress.com

March 2019

This book is part of the *Critical Pedagogies* Series

Series Editor: Shirley R. Steinberg

Dedication

This book is dedicated to Alison E. Hayes, and to all lesbian, gay, bisexual, transgender, and queer (LGBTQ) children, youth, couples, and families past, present, and future in Taiwan, the USA, and worldwide deserving affirmation, love, hope, legal equity, and the strength to challenge hate with love.

Acknowledgements

This book began 12 years ago inspired by my first sabbatical in Taiwan teaching at National Changhua University of Education in the Spring of 2007. At that time, I taught a section of doctoral students and my husband, Dr. Lance Chen-Hayes, and I co-taught a bilingual section of master's students in Taiwan's first sexuality counseling classes. As far as I know, it was the only time in Asia a gay male couple has co-taught a graduate course. Dr. Sharon (Shu-chu) Chao, professor of counseling and at the time, Dean of Education, asked if I would consider writing the story of our family in English and the result is on these pages. Dr. Leigh Harbin provided excellent suggestions to strengthen the manuscript and fabulous friendship. Also, thanks to Dr. Ian Levy, Manhattan College, my school counselor education colleague in the Bronx, who connected me with DIO Press. I am grateful to the DIO Press founders, CEO Michel Lokhorst, and the chance to share my family memoir in English with an international readership. My husband Lance and I are finalizing a Mandarin-language book sharing our story through his eyes as lead author: "兩個爸爸恰恰好: 台美同志家庭拓荒之旅." Lance's feedback on *Double Dads* has been thoughtful, supportive, and constant. Thanks to the Bih family for help in publishing the Mandarin-language book and ensuring the Chen-Hayes family story is accessible to Mandarin readers worldwide. Last, I cherish my CUNY Lehman College colleagues, students, and alumni in the Bronx and beyond who have given thoughtful feedback and support along the way, particularly Sexuality Counseling class participants.

Note to Mandarin readers on the English edition and forthcoming Mandarin edition

Welcome to the English edition of our family story. The journey to publication has been a long one and parallels the extraordinary political changes in both the USA and Taiwan regarding LGBTQ rights, LGBTQ parenting, and marriage equality. There are two versions of this story: the English version written from my perspective as a USA citizen hoping to be a Taiwan permanent resident through gay marriage, is here published by DIO Press, Inc. A second version will be published in Mandarin in 2020 with a Taiwan-based publisher co-authored with my husband Lance in the lead as Taiwan's first out gay father. The nuances of growing up gay in Taiwan and becoming a dual-national family are shared in Mandarin. Updates will be posted on Chen-Haye's Facebook page and on Stuart's Twitter account @schenhayes.

給中文讀者：

我們這個同志家庭拓荒之旅的故事終於出書了。原本以為中文版會先出書的，沒想到英文版倒是先出了。這本書出版的過程充滿困難和曲折，似乎也呼應了同志族群在美國與台灣爭取婚姻和其他平等權利的荊棘之路。

我們決定將我們的故事以兩種不同版本，分別用英文和中文出版。英文版是思鐸多年來累積資料慢慢寫成的，這是以一個想入台灣籍的美國人的觀點，來敘說我們跨國跨種族的故事，這本英文書是由紐約市的DIO出版社在2019年出版。中文版則由子良執筆，根據思鐸所彙集的資料，重新寫出子良自己的歷程和我們家庭的故事。我們希望這個以台灣人的經驗寫成的中文版，能夠讓中文讀者產生更大的共鳴。這本中文書預計在2020年由台灣的出版社出書。

我們會用社交媒體發佈任何最新訊息，請到陳子良的臉書（Lance Chen-Hayes）和陳海思鐸的推特（@schenhayes）追尋詳情。

About the Author

Stuart F. Chen-Hayes is Professor of Counselor Education in the Counseling, Leadership, Literacy, and Special Education department in the School of Education at Lehman College of the City University of New York (CUNY). A native of Park Forest, IL, he holds a B.A. in Journalism and Religious Studies and an M.S.Ed. in Counseling and Counselor Education from Indiana University and a Ph.D. in Counselor Education from Kent State University. He has experience as a professional counselor and consultant in addiction, college student affairs, couple and family, mental health, middle school, and sexuality counseling settings in multiple states in the USA. He is the co-author of *101 Solutions for School Counselors and Leaders in Challenging Times* (Corwin Press). He and his husband have co-authored the forthcoming 兩個爸爸恰恰好：台美同志家庭拓荒之旅 "Two Dads are Just Fine" in Mandarin. The author of multiple peer-reviewed book chapters and research articles and presenter of over 250 social justice and counseling presentations, Dr. Chen-Hayes co-founded Counselors for Social Justice, worked closely with the White House College Access/School Counseling Convenings when Michelle Obama was First Lady, has received over $1.2 million in research grants, and his current research and scholarship are focused on college access and affordability and sexuality counseling. As for service, he is active in union organizing and anti-privatization movements in public education with the online international group @TeachSolidarity and fighting for pay parity for City University of New York (CUNY) adjunct faculty with @CUNYStruggle and the PSC-CUNY union. He was elected Judge of Elections in Newtown Township, PA and is also active with SAVE Bucks Votes and the successful 2016 Dr. Jill Stein lawsuit against Pennsylvania's archaic voting recount laws, which has led to the state being required to use secure, verifiable, easily audited paper ballots in all polling places. His retirement goal is to open a Dog Rescue/Bubble Tea Cafe run by homeless LGBTQ persons in Taipei modeled on the work of Glenn Greenwald and David Miranda in Rio de Janeiro, Brazil.

Table of Contents

Appendices

A. Sacred Commitment Ceremony Program (Chicago, IL)

B. Gay Wedding & 15-year Renewal of Vows Program (NYC, NY)

C. #FIRSTGAYTEENDAY Order of Ceremony and 30 Ritual

Messages (Asbury Park, NJ)

CHAPTER ONE

SPRING ROLLS & DADDY DREAMS

CHICAGO FIRST DATE

Two gay men usually don't discuss dreams of being dads on a first date. For most couples, regardless of sexual orientation, there are usually other things on their minds and racing through their bodies. But, as a couple, we have been nonconformists since we came out of the closet years ago, so why would our first date differ? It was freezing, sub-zero cold with Lake Michigan-influenced wind chills around the dinner hour on a dark January 22, 1995 in Chicago and we had talked on the phone nightly for a week prior. We had found each other through a personal ad in the *Chicago Reader*, a progressive arts and culture paper in Chicago where the technological advance in dating at the time was leaving a voicemail message to express interest in one's potential date.

Little did I know that Lance Chen (Chen-Tzyy Liang) had friends in from New York City that weekend and they reviewed all the messages and decided hands down that I won the prize. During our introductory week of nightly phone conversations prior to our first date, I shared that I was concerned about one phrase Lance had used in his personal ad about traditional values (would nonconformity be in danger, I wondered?). Fortunately, I guessed accurately that Lance honored his cultural traditions and appreciated many aspects about his family (we shared a commitment to the strengths of extended families and appreciating ethnic/racial identities). Lance wanted to ensure that I was not a "rice queen," i.e., a White gay man exclusively attracted to Asians. I shared that I was attracted to all ethnic/racial identities and I wanted to make sure Lance was not a "potato queen," an Asian gay man exclusively attracted to White people. He was not.

Lance shared a mutual interest in attraction to men of all ethnic/racial identities and was equally turned off by the racist "White is right, Asian is not" mentality in the gay community at that time (it has improved somewhat but the dynamic is still flourishes in many European-oriented gay venues where Asians are treated in racist ways including not being allowed to enter) for many of our Asian and White gay brothers (i.e., the infamous rice queen/potato queen dilemma—we had opted for none of the above in our dating histories—or actually all of the above and everyone else, too, please). I, too, was readying a personal ad to put in *The Reader*, Chicago's equivalent of the *Village Voice*, just before I placed the message response to his ad in Lance's voicemail box. A few weeks later, I mailed the personal ad to Lance saying that I didn't think I would need it anymore (although I did later assist the woman who lived across the way from me in our condo building with her personal ad and Karianne Soulsby ended up happily married to her happy heterosexual catch. What are gay neighbors for but a little wordsmithing at just the right moment?)

Lance, upon receiving and reading my personal ad, said it was too racy and that he never would have responded to it. But one ad was all we needed. It turned out we lived about a mile from each other on Chicago's North side. I picked up Lance for a dinner date and drove to a Vietnamese restaurant in Uptown (ordering both egg rolls and spring rolls for appetizers) called the Mekong (which sadly closed its doors only a few years later so we had to find an alternative anniversary location for our first date restaurant). But better the Mekong restaurant out of business than us as a couple. One thing we hadn't talked about all week was that both of us were interested in being dads. Lance had never thought about the possibility of being a dad as a gay man. But the more he thought it over, the more he now saw it as a possibility but not right away. Later Lance shared how my posing that question "really rocked his world." He and I both had never dreamed we would consider parenthood due to the homophobia we were both surrounded with growing up in the USA and Taiwan. Lance wanted to wait before considering parenthood, however, to work out some job and career issues first. I was fine with that and thrilled to know that it was a definite possibility down the road for him (and us). Maybe there were some traditional components to us, after all. Something clicked that night for both of us. I remember feeling attracted not only physically to Lance but that there was a remarkable sense of connection on all the issues we had talked about--politics, culture, family, friends, and shared interests. We were both so excited to have finally met after a week of phone calls where we hit it off verbally. In-person was even better. What sealed the deal? It must have been the two-hour kiss in the car where we nearly ended up with frostbitten fingers and toes with a -22F windchill. We've been together ever since. But prior meeting, our lives had different beginnings 8,000 miles apart with unique and shared elements prior to coming out gay and making our way across the planet.

Lance Chen-Hayes was born Chen Tzyy-Liang, the youngest son of nine siblings, seven sons and two daughters, in Taichung, Taiwan with parents who were a police officer and a homemaker. Lance's mother was the only child of a traditional Chinese Medical/Herbal Doctor and a fabric store owner. Lance's maternal grandparents were highly respected in their hometown, a seaside village in China's south-eastern Fujian Province. But because Lance's mom was an only child, Lance's father was asked to marry "into" Lance's mother's family through an arranged marriage to help carry her family name. So, Lance's five eldest siblings bear the family name of Hsiao (Lance's mother's side) while the last four bear the family name of Chen (Lance's father's side). Lance's parents and grandparents fled to Taichung, Taiwan in the mid 1940's right as the Communist Party took over China.

The family was robbed of all material possessions in China at this beginning of the communist revolution and the end of World War II. The Hsiao/Chen family had no alternative but to start from the ground up in Taiwan. Lance's dad supported the family with a police officer's salary and benefits. Even with little in the way of material possessions (including one toy as a child), Lance grew up in a working-class family with a high value on education for his generation as a way up the economic ladder.

Lance started to notice his attraction to other boys when he was in about 6th grade. He always did well academically at school but fared poorly in sports. Fortunately, with Taiwan an academically oriented culture, Lance was seldom teased for his lack of prowess in sports. Instead, he was appreciated and admired by his teachers and peers for his academic skills. However, under this glossy "good student" façade, Lance started to hide his deepest secret of being attracted to other boys. When he was in junior high school, to find an answer to his difference, Lance secretly studied his sister's medical books as she was in nursing school at the time.

When he read "homosexuality was a psychiatric disorder" he was mortified. He vowed to hide his secret forever and to change himself with all his might. During his freshman year in college, Lance was approached by Campus Crusade missionaries and converted from his family's Presbyterianism (originally Buddhist) to evangelical Christianity. With the promise of a "new life," Lance eagerly participated in varied evangelical Christian activities. He took on many leadership roles in the church and in the Campus Crusade movement, and he converted many classmates to Christianity. Lance also developed a relationship with a woman from his class (after many nights of praying for a "sign" from God if he should proceed with her pursuit). While the "new life" blossomed on the surface, Lance knew his inner struggle never had stopped. There were many nights when he locked himself in a "prayer room" and cried because he could not stop his physical attraction to men.

The more Lance tried to suppress his sexuality, the stronger his attraction toward men grew. When Lance was finally away from the church serving in the Taiwanese military, he had the time and space to find clarity about his attractions and desires. Lance renounced Christianity a few years later and chose a spiritual path closer to Buddhism, his family's original spiritual background. After his first sexual encounter with another man toward the end of his military service, Lance came out to himself and to his almost-ready-to-get-married girlfriend as gay. Although the truth and subsequent break-up were painful for both, they remained good friends. However, coming out as a gay man in Taiwan in the late 80's was difficult. There were gay bars, cruising parks, and bathhouses for gay men to socialize in but most gay men were closeted outside those venues and rarely did anyone speak of gay people or gay relationships in family settings or the media, and if they were mentioned, it was always derogatory.

There were few resources for LGBTQ folks to develop positive attitudes and support in Taiwan at that time. Lance struggled with internalized heterosexism while navigating new emotional territory. A few years later, he decided to immigrate to the USA for graduate school in a work-study program in physical therapy at New York University after finishing his bachelor's degree at National Taiwan University in Taipei. After arriving in New York City in 1990, he adjusted well to the competing demands of graduate school, a new job, language and cultural differences, and emotional and social isolation as a closeted gay international student of color who spoke English with an accent. After treading carefully for a year, Lance went to his first Gay Pride Parade in NYC and was changed forever. Being surrounded with so many diverse gay people in such large numbers celebrating pride empowered Lance. He started to participate more in the LGBTQ community and developed a positive attitude about being gay and coming out socially. He became involved in the gay Asian community and learned about the complex oppression issues that gay Asian and Pacific Islanders faced in the USA and abroad. For example, he quickly noticed how images of gay Asian and Pacific Islander men were few and far between in gay venues, let alone in the corporate and alternative media. He also learned the ropes of being in long-term relationships with men and dated men of different ethnic and cultural backgrounds.

A few months before we met, Lance ended an abusive relationship with a gay white man who abused alcohol and who was emotionally, physically, and financially abusive. They had met in New York and the man had convinced Lance to move to Chicago. But on the trip as they moved to Chicago, the soon-to-be-ex boyfriend declared that he wanted to end the relationship (but still wanted to control Lance's life). Lance was furious but had no choice but to stay in the same apartment that they had rented prior to the trip to Chicago. But ending the dating relationship didn't stop the problems. The most chilling moment in his life came when his ex-boyfriend came home drunk one night and attempted to strangle him. The conversation that preceded the ex-boyfriend's rageful attack was when Lance stated that he was planning to date other people and to resume a regular social life without the ex-boyfriend. Like any abusive relationship, this threatened the ex-boyfriend's perceived power and control over Lance. At that time, after months of living with a man who continued to be emotionally and financially abusive, even after the relationship had ended, Lance was too drained to fight back as the ex-boyfriend lunged for his neck.

Lance felt like he was going to die during the attack and that he was losing his will to live.

When the ex-boyfriend realized that he had almost killed Lance, he let loose of Lance's neck. Lance grabbed a few things and immediately went to a friend's apartment to stay temporarily. The next day he contacted the landlord, explained the situation, and the landlord graciously took Lance's name off the lease. Lance learned a lot about relationship violence from his abusive ex-boyfriend. He had not had any background or knowledge about abusive relationship dynamics and thought that his job was to help maintain the relationship. But coming close to being killed was not part of the bargain. Since that time, Lance has been an outspoken advocate raising awareness about interpersonal violence in same-gender male and other relationships.

I was born the eldest of two siblings to a former botany professor of Scottish ethnicity who hailed from a middle-class family raised in Buffalo, NY and a high school teacher and part-time flight instructor/pilot of English ethnicity raised in a working-class family in rural southern Indiana descended from John and Priscilla Alden who crossed from England on the Mayflower. I remember being attracted to both boys and girls at an early age. I grew up in the south Chicago suburb of Park Forest and was a horribly failed heterosexual. The other kids figured this out well before I was willing to admit it as I was a gender-variant boy, and I was teased mercilessly in elementary school without any adult intervention. I was mortified to tell anyone what was happening, including regular physical assaults on the way home from school and daily verbal abuse during and after school. My gender variance made me visibly different from the other boys and I was an easy target for victimization in a town full of "organization men," post-World War II veterans and their wives and children mostly seeking to get ahead in the rat race where conformity to gender norms and heterosexuality were keys to success.

I developed a first crush on a girl (harpist Lisa Tannebaum)—but the attraction was primarily intellectual and a competition with her to see who could get the highest A+ grade on Mrs. Gilchrist's sixth grade history tests at Indiana elementary school. My parents were educators--intellectual, introverted, and isolated from family who were in either Southern Indiana or New York state other than their mothers, who lived with us or nearby for many years, and we were unique among our neighbors for our interests in books, the environment, the arts, and current events. Middle school at Huth Upper Grades Center in Matteson, IL, was a better experience, as it was my first chance to find other nerdy kids who were more into the arts than sports. As an extrovert, I enjoyed a large social network for the first time. I developed definite crushes on several boys in class and the teasing from elementary school was reduced due to connecting with other kids who valued me for my intelligence and interest in the arts, student council, drama club, reader's theatre, the school plays, band (oboe), and chorus. Other than the obnoxious kids on the bus ride to and from school and dreaded gym class, it was a better school experience, especially with the chance to perform in arts activities where I excelled. I had a couple of platonic dates with girls to school dances and kept my crushes on boys hidden and unrequited.

But the middle school fed into two different high schools and I was mortified that most of my newfound friends were off to rival Rich Central high school in Olympia Fields, IL, and I was back with the abusive kids from elementary school at Rich South high school in Richton Park, IL. I did find a few new friends, and I was a strong student, but I spent most of my time with after-school activities like concert, jazz, and marching bands, writing and co-editing the school newspaper, *The Centurion,* and working concessions, box office, and occasional bit parts in shows at the local Equity (actors union) professional theater company, The Illinois Theatre Center before I left Illinois for college. I didn't date at all in high school. But I did have my first sexual experience with another boy and that confirmed for me that I was attracted to males. I didn't act on that again until my first year of graduate school, but as an actor, I had the skills to keep that part of me under wraps, or so I thought. My undergraduate years at Indiana University included the social interaction I missed in high school, and initially I didn't spend as much time on my studies as I could have. Perhaps the funniest part of my early college experience was being "converted" into the God Squad briefly at the end of my freshman year by conservative Christians. Fortunately, a summer at home after that experience had me practically laughed out of my parents' house, so when I returned to college my sophomore year, I decided to do a double major and study world religions. But this delayed my coming out as I looked toward different religions for answers about my sexuality that did not exist. I did some dating, too, but only a few women--and nothing very sexual. I graduated on time with a degree in journalism and religious studies, experience as a reporter for three years with the *Indiana Daily Student* and as a resident assistant for two years, and happy to have developed a group of close friends.

But I wasn't ready to leave Bloomington, Indiana just yet. Exiting the closet had to wait until my first year of graduate school at age 21 at Indiana University when I started a master's degree in counseling and began my journey as bisexual. My coming out experience that year began with my sister, who was supportive, and then my parents whose support included my mother's first response, which was, "I think I might be bisexual, too!" I didn't know what to say to that but never forgot her first reaction. I studied sexuality counseling with the late Dr. Alan Bell, the former Kinsey Institute psychologist. I attended a Sexual Attitude Reassessment (SAR) weekend as part of the course, which helped hasten my debut in the queer world. But I eventually failed bisexuality, too, (although I was good at it for about a decade) after a couple of relationships with women and brief flings with men in between while I worked as a residence hall director and part-time group counselor at Cornell University in Ithaca, NY. The first woman I dated was also bisexual and later married a man. But the second woman I dated left me for another woman (who knew!). We remain friends, and enjoy the coincidence of how our lives intersected. I had wanted to be in a relationship and at that time women were open to that and sex; the men I met were only interested in sex. I was aware I had stronger attractions to men; my attractions to women (other than friendship) went into permanent decline. I then moved to Riverside, RI, where I commuted daily to work as a part-time adolescent and family crisis hospital diversion counselor and a part-time middle school counselor in Fall River and Westport, MA. At this time I managed my first political actions in the gay world in Providence, RI, which included testifying in favor of gay rights at the statehouse, dating a coupe of gay men, and landing my first boyfriend in a long-term, long-distance relationship in the San Francisco bay area just as I was accepted to and the Ph.D. program in Counselor Education specializing in family and multicultural counseling at Kent State University in Kent, OH, and a move back to the midwest.

My doctoral work was with three powerful women including two Counselor Education professors, Dr. Anita Jackson and the late Dr. Mary Smith Arnold, who challenged me on multiple issues of unlearning oppression including racism, sexism, and heterosexism. They taught me ethnic/racial identity development and world view models, and helped push my learning about privilege and power in my identity development as a White bisexual man. Dr. Jackson and I created the first sexuality counseling course at Kent State University as well as the first advanced multicultural counseling course. My Ph.D. clinical internship was with feminist psychiatrist/sex therapist Victoria Codispoti, M.D., who prepared me well for future adventures in challenging oppressions professionally and personally working with a wide range of individuals, couples, and families in her practice with issues from sexual orientation to gender identity to survivors and perpetrators of sexual abuse. At the end of my time at Kent, I made two moves: I took a first job as an assistant professor of counselor education at a small private university in metropolitan Chicago, and I acknowledged that I had lost all sexual attraction and fantasies about women. I came out again, this time as gay, about three weeks to the day before I met Lance on our first date. But with the success of our first week of phone calls and that promising first date, we had no idea where we were headed personally or geographically, let alone how we would finance or support a future child.

CHAPTER TWO

BALANCING ACTIVISM, WORLD VIEWS, & 2 SETS OF FURNITURE

We fell in love--not at first sight, but after a few weeks (we both were wary having been burned in the past) and we clicked due to a shared interest in social justice projects. Lance began work with gay Asians and Pacific Islanders in Chicago in GAPIC, a group founded by transgender activist Pauline Park (prior to her transition as Pauline), I-Li Hsiao, Sam Chiu, Joe Mendoza, and Gerry Arrieta. Lance became a Gay Asians and Pacific Islanders of Chicago (GAPIC) co-chair. He was involved in varied actions, demonstrations, and parades to raise Queer and Asian consciousness in Chicago. During that time, Lance helped organize Chicago's first coalition of Asian Pacific Islander South Asians of Chicago (APISAC), which included lesbians, bisexuals, and persons of transgender and gender-variant experience in addition to gay men.

GAPIC was unique in Chicago because it was the first gay Asian group focused on affirming gay Asians. It counterbalanced the "Asians and Friends" movement that often paired White men who were often racist with Asian men with internalized racism who undervalued themselves as Asian and overvalued White men as attractive and excluded other ethnic and racial identities. GAPIC members went a different direction. They affirmed gay Asian men as fully human, erotic, and intelligent beings who could date other Asians or whomever else they wanted to of any ethnic/racial identity without stereotypes and colonized, racist dynamics.

I became involved with a group called the Color Triangle in Chicago, and helped with anti-racism and ally work within the transgender community. But our activism was not always by choice. We developed a crash-course for ourselves in challenging the effects of gay interpersonal violence. Lance had only had relationships with other Asians until his prior relationship with a gay white man who abused alcohol and Lance. Although Lance had left the relationship and moved out immediately after a physical assault, the ex-boyfriend-from-hell tried to find Lance once soon after we started dating. Lance called me saying his ex-boyfriend was pounding on his apartment door. In response, I took the fastest car ride of my life to Lance's place, found he was safe, and encouraged Lance to call the police.

When I arrived, there was no sign of the ex, who likely heard Lance on the phone and decided to make himself scarce. When a Chicago police officer arrived after what seemed an eternity, we encountered our first experience of linguicism and heterosexism as a couple. The officer who responded was male, Asian, likely heterosexual, and spoke standard English. He didn't listen to Lance or his concerns and misunderstood what had occurred. He had difficulty making the connections that men who loved men could also be violent with other men in terms of abuse and interpersonal violence. We weren't sure if he had any training or background in working with interpersonal violence or with gay people, and we resented having to educate him on the spot. I spoke using privilege as a white male mental health professional and the officer seemed to see the seriousness of the threat. We wondered if we had been heterosexual if the officer would have responded similarly. Fortunately, Lance's ex never made another appearance. We saw the importance of educating others in LGBTQ communities about interpersonal violence and recognized that Chicago's "finest" needed help, too.

Next, in an attempt to build community, we decided to join the Second Unitarian church on Chicago's north side when we heard that they were involved in the anti-racist multicultural movement and open to all faiths. But as the token Asian and White gay couple we found a lot of well-meaning White liberals but not much affirmation. There were some children of color in the basement (where the Sunday school operated), but most had been adopted by White parents (which was ok, but the congregation was "generationally challenged" in terms of racial diversity. We recognized the pattern of segregation in most houses of worship in the United States and dreamed of a different path. The experience at Second Unitarian felt more like work for us (except for singing in the choir, which was always the best part!). Lance had felt early on that it was not a good fit, that something was not quite right. I learned over time that Lance was often more attuned to the subtleties of racism as a man of color. I also learned that Lance was upset that I wasn't always clear about the subtleties of racism, and I needed to recognize more of my White privilege and be a more observant ally. We made a few friends there, although we ended our journey after about a year as fallen Unitarians, just like my parents several decades earlier (they met in a Unitarian-Universalist church in southern Indiana, although my dad was never a member and mom eventually went on to other spiritual pursuits, too, a mix of Hinduism and Christianity—it was no wonder I studied comparative world religions in college).

After 11 months of dating in 1995, we had clicked emotionally, physically, spiritually, and politically as a couple and we were excited at our decision to move in together. Lance joined me in a small two-bedroom condo on the north side of Chicago in the Uptown neighborhood near the intersection of Kenmore Avenue and Irving Park Road that I purchased in March of 1994. But with two 30-something gay men, we had a challenge— two sets of everything and 800 square feet. Somehow, we managed and merged our possessions with the help of my parents' garage and basement, and a year later we decided it was time to find a larger place and to combine finances. We had our "gay engagement" party at "The Melba," our first address on Kenmore Avenue, and Lance did his best to adjust to my overly loyal Sheltie, Hermes, whom we took to puppy school as an adult dog to help him transition another man in the household.

During our time together, we balanced modern and traditional worldviews, Asian and White European-American, which meant that Lance, as an introvert who spoke Mandarin, Taiwanese, Fujianese, and English, was a man of few words, and I, an extroverted speaker of English, spoke a lot of words all the time. We learned, as I had been taught by Mary Smith Arnold and her "Unlearning Oppression" workshops, to "fall in love with the difference" and appreciated each other's linguistic and personality skills.

When things got tense for us as a couple, we used our Asian and European worldviews to our advantage. For example, Lance would often be more collectivist in his approach to problem-solving employing a "both-and" and consensus-building approach, and I learned to lessen my individualistic "either-or" focus over time. Another area of difference for us in disagreements was the indirect and direct communication styles between traditional Asian and European worldviews. Lance would often think to himself, "Stuart, GET TO THE POINT!" Sometimes I would say to Lance, "Use more words, I don't understand!"

When Lance discussed the importance of sending money home to support Taiwanese parents (with no social security in Taiwan, children are traditional parents' social security), I readily agreed. I felt that this was something that would help cement our relationship as a couple and as a part of Lance's family. As a couple, we were often asked early in our relationship about how we divvied up tasks at home. Unlike heterosexual couples, we didn't have any gender roles that made us assign tasks. We, like many same-gender couples, chose to assign tasks based on who was better at what. We both cook, but my repertoire consisted of about five USA dishes that were repeated weekly. Lance, however, liked to cook five nights a week from scratch because it relaxed him and he never repeated a dish, so he was an easy winner for food preparation and that relegated me to clean-up duty and household entertainer. Lance hated how I folded clothes and with his required Taiwan military training after high school and before college, he racked up laundry. We split cleaning and I did banking, most errands, grocery shopping, social scheduling, and phone calls due to my flexible work schedule as a professor. But there was another reason I was the one mostly on the phone in English. Lance had studied English for years in Taiwan, and his skill with English was as good if not better than most native speakers. But leave it to some conservative USA sales people to freak out over the phone when they heard Lance's accent. Some would just hang up or say rude things. So we agreed that I would take the primary calls at home so that Lance could avoid the nasty linguicism targeting him. Ironically, it took me almost two years to learn how to pronounce Lance's Taiwanese name correctly using accurate tones in Mandarin, just in time for the next stage of our flowering courtship, including a surprise family coming out and a once-in-a-lifetime meeting between our parents.

CHAPTER THREE

TAIWANUS TOGETHER

THE 8,000-MILE ENGAGEMENT

Just after we moved in together at my Chicago condo, we made our first visit as a couple to Taiwan in December of 1995 and January of 1996. We stayed for most of the trip with Lance's parents in Taichung, the third largest city in Taiwan with the highlight our gay engagement at Sun-Moon Lake in the central Taiwan mountains. Later, we held the second part of our gay engagement back in the USA atop the John Hancock building in Chicago. We decided early on to buy gay engagement rings together and that we would both ask each other: Will you "Mary" me? Since we didn't have traditional marriage as an option, we decided to use the campy gay term for men and figured being "Mary'd" reflected our interest in pair-bonding without the sexist connotations of marriage. We had the chance to create a loving partnership on our own terms and kept traditional elements that honored us and discarded those that didn't fit. Lance and I were excited that we had finally found the one man who was worth the wait.

We planned on "TAIWANUS" together so that both of us could pop the question on his home turf. We also took advantage of a brief side trip to Hong Kong and visited sights in both Taiwan and Hong Kong and included extended time in Taipei, where we stayed with one of Lance's brothers and family. We also did our first invited LGBTQ couple workshop presentation on gay and lesbian couple issues at a small LGBTQ-friendly coffeehouse in Taipei, the Locomotion Café, for an all-lesbian audience. Lance had learned about the venue and contacted the owners, who insisted that we do a presentation on being an out-of-the-closet, gay, mixed-race, dual-national, bilingual couple.

We were honored to talk about our activism and our young relationship at that time. For Lance, it was exciting to see gay life beginning to arise (in Taipei, at least) in cafes, bookstores, literary circles, and public lectures, a different story from the Taiwan under repressive martial law he had left a few years earlier that relegated gay life to the margins of karaoke bars, saunas, parks, and little public recognition or affirmation. Before this trip, Lance had planned on coming out to his parents but he delayed the news. On the last night of our first trip as a couple in Taiwan, Lance's mom came to the bedroom of her Taichung townhouse that she had prepared for us to stay in. She looked at Lance as if she had a lot of questions to ask and a lot to say, but she said nothing. Instead, she cried and Lance cried with her as if there was an implicit understanding that we were more than friends, although it was unspoken.

Prior to this, Lance had struggled with coming out to his family during his 20s. He had come out to himself as a gay man in the Taiwanese military (mandatory two years of service at the time) and left behind a wonderful dating relationship with a woman who loved him deeply, as he did her, but he could not live a lie any longer. We talked at length about coming out and

Lance felt no pressure from me—we both realized that in Taiwanese culture coming out was a challenge and rarely done at that time. That didn't stop Lance's desire to do so. We had both seen filmmaker Ang Lee's "The Wedding Banquet" just before we met, and we knew it was based in part on a true story between a Taiwanese gay man and a White European-American gay man. But the movie, while humorous, didn't provide many clues about how to be open and honest with Taiwanese parents.

Lance first came out to two of his siblings whom he thought would be the most supportive. While they were affirming, that was not enough to satisfy Lance's desire to be honest and open. Before our first trip to Taiwan as a couple, Lance was determined to come out to his whole family, especially his parents. Lance did what traditional sons do in a culture honoring filial piety. He wrote a 24-page (ten-thousand Mandarin characters) letter home to his eight siblings and asked for their permission and blessing to come out as gay to his mom and dad. Lance's siblings had a first-ever family meeting to discuss his coming-out letter. Most supported Lance's being gay. But they decided that Lance should not come out to their parents for fear of their parents' inability to handle the news at their advanced age. Lance reluctantly and unhappily agreed to their wishes.

So we went on our first trip to Taiwan as "friends" in Lance's parents' eyes, but everyone else in the family knew what was up with us as a couple. However, our appearance in person did nothing to stop Lance's mom from speculating about "her baby." She knew, as most savvy parents do. After we left Taiwan and returned to the USA, Lance's mom questioned Lance's sisters if Lance was gay. Up until a trip back to Taiwan being interviewed for a documentary film, Lance was told by his mom that his sister #2 had told his mother about his being gay. (With siblings in Taiwan it is tradition to refer to them by birth order rather than their first names and as the youngest of nine, Lance is brother #7). That was incorrect. It turns out his eldest Sister #1 had told Lance's mom due to intense pressure she was feeling from the rest of the siblings. When Lance heard the news that his sister had spilled the beans (although at the time he thought it was sister # 2), he was furious that he had been outed by a sibling to his mom.

I had a different reaction. I thought it was a gift. I reframed it with the realization that he had half of what he wanted (coming out to his mom) without betraying the agreement with his siblings. Lance came around to this view quickly. When Lance's mom found out the truth, she experienced repeated feelings of sadness, anger, hurt, guilt, and resignation over the span of a few months. But in less than a year, she was at peace having accepted her son as gay and her "American son" and Lance as a couple. The few months when Lance's mom was on an emotional roller coaster were not easy for Lance, in part, because the communication was weekly by phone at a distance of 8,000 miles. But Lance persisted and reminded himself that his mother's upset would pass. On many an occasion she has reminded him by phone and in person in Taichung that he was her favorite child. He continued to make weekly calls home to mom to let her know that he would always be her son and that he loved her even when she was angry and hurt.

With the help of some supportive siblings in Taiwan talking to his mom to help her understand and accept Lance as gay, she finally adjusted her emotions and prepared for her and her husband's first trip to the USA to visit us in Chicago. Lance's parents had planned the trip in advance before she found out Lance was gay and in a relationship with me. Now the challenge for her became how to conceal from her husband the fact that we were gay (and out, loud, and proud) when they came to visit. She did not want to tell Lance's dad about this for fear it would harm his emotional and physical health or that he might take it out on her.

We flew from Chicago to San Francisco to meet Lance's parents' plane from Taiwan and toured the city of San Francisco with them for a long weekend prior to bringing them to Chicago. We enjoyed the irony of a gay couple touring one set of parents around one of the gayest cities in the USA on their first weekend in the states. We visited various Bay Area sites including an excellent Hakkanese restaurant, Japantown, Chinatown, and various parks and museums. Lance's mom had the chance to practice what she would say to Lance's dad for a few weeks before they arrived at our new condo on Argyle St. in Chicago's Uptown neighborhood. On day number two at home in Chicago, Lance's dad asked Lance's mom if I was gay. Since Taiwan is an indirect culture, Lance's dad would never have asked about his own son directly. Lance's mom was all prepared and responded with the three sentences she had planned and earlier rehearsed by phone with Lance:

- "Oh, they're just weird (or queer in Mandarin)." We couldn't have put it better ourselves.
- "They don't want to get married." This was true legally at the time as we could not get married, although we certainly wanted equal rights.
- "They plan to spend the rest of their lives together and take care of each other."

Lance's dad accepted this answer and did not ask any more questions. Lance's dad asked indirectly and Lance's mom responded indirectly without "lying." Everyone was satisfied. Without using the label gay, Lance's dad accepted the situation of his son and his "American son" more easily. The label gay was laden with negative stereotypes and feelings for some elders in Taiwanese culture; using it, at the time, would have made it hard to see past the label and accept LGBTQ offspring. Lance's mom created an indirect and honest way for gay Asians to come out to traditional parents. We had made the decision to not make any changes to our home decor (gay artwork, homoerotic pictures, and each room was painted for a color of the rainbow in softer hues) for Lance's parents' arrival. We thought, "We're here, we're queer, and we're not de-gaying our place." In fact, Lance's parents loved the time they spent in the USA with us, particularly the neighborhood, which reminded them of home in the city of Taichung. We had bought our first condo together a block from Lake Michigan in Chicago's uptown neighborhood on Argyle St., a Scottish name that had become the central East-West street in the north side Asian town with many Vietnamese and Chinese restaurants, groceries, and other small businesses, which allowed Lance's parents to easily walk to shops and restaurants with Mandarin publications, signs, menus, and East Asian people, food, and culture.

This trip was also the only time that our parents met. We took advantage of their proximity and they had the chance to meet several times over the course of Lance's parents' visit. The most memorable meeting for all six of us was lunch in the 95th restaurant atop the John Hancock building on a picture-perfect day. My father had retired from being a part-time flight instructor and private pilot, so he especially enjoyed being up in the sky. Although neither set of parents could speak the other language, our moms communicated well with body language and our dads were, as usual, stoic and quiet. Both moms complimented each other on how beautiful each other looked. With the successful visit of Lance's parents to the USA, and the subsequent meeting of our parents, it was time to move ahead with details on staging our sacred commitment ceremony--the "illegal" wedding. From handmade invitations and original vows, we combined elements of Taiwanese, Mandarin, English, and Scottish ethnic and linguistic and gay identities and united two families 8,000 miles apart.

CHAPTER FOUR

THE "ILLEGAL" WEDDING

JUST MARY'D & THE QUEERMOON

It was the hottest wedding in the summer of 1997. June in Chicago was usually warm but the day of our sacred commitment ceremony it was unusually steamy inside and outside the Second Unitarian Church sanctuary on tree-lined Barry Street nestled among condos and apartments in the heart of Chicago's Boystown neighborhood. The detail we overlooked in planning? The Tudor-style church had no air-conditioning, few windows, and it was 88 degrees in the shade at 11:00 a.m. on June 28.

As celebrants walked the narrow sidewalks into the church foyer they were greeted by the sounds of Scottish bagpipes honoring half of my ethnic heritage while my Indiana University classmate Leigh Harbin distributed the oversize program of service with deep purple corrugated paper tied with silver glitter-string ensconcing several pages of lavender parchment with Black cursive script announcing the proceedings. Attendees immediately put them to good use as fans to make it through *un*-air-conditioned Chicago humidity and heat. Heading further into the sanctuary guests were greeted by a gaggle of extra-tall Radical Faeries prancing about in fabulous frocks, high heels, and a variety of summer bonnets to mark the festivities. As attendees were seated in the sanctuary their gaze came to rest at the altar, which had one fierce 8-foot tall bouquet lovingly created by floral designer and API queer activist I-Li Hsiao enveloping the church with the fragrance of fresh-cut Asian lilies and varied European-American flower varieties of purple and white surrounded with lush greenery. Also on the altar were a large round rainbow candle and two hand-blown glass goblets filled with grapefruit juice and Elderflower--the cups of bitterness and sweetness used in medieval same-gender commitment ceremonies uncovered by the late gay historian John Boswell.

And speaking of giddiness, our flower girl, Jerry Hsieh, flirted and danced down the runway in a full extra-virgin white wedding-ball gown with headdress drag blowing kisses, working her white faux cell phone, and strewing purple and pink flower petals over the crowd with a flourish flinging final petals atop the head of my father as Cyndi Lauper's "*Girls just wanna have fun*" set the tone for the rest of the ceremony. The guardian angels sashayed their way into the sanctuary and took their seats just before we made our grand entrance, each with bouquet in hand, singing, dancing, and waving to the crowd with our hands in matching princess waves walking down the aisle to the tune of Bette Midler's "Chapel of Love."

Then, minister Rev. Roger Jones commenced the ceremony with wit, care, and reverence counterbalancing our flamboyance. We included varied traditional rituals such as lighting of a unity candle, the traditional Taiwanese bowing to elders for thanking parents (Stuart's parents Lois and Charlie and Lance's parents represented by his next eldest brother Chun Chen and our niece Linda Hsiao) and family blessings, and lighting incense to honor the ancestors. We also included two readings from the work of lesbian warrior of color poet Audre Lorde:

"Difference must be not merely tolerated, but seen as a fund of necessary polarities between which our creativity can spark like a dialectic. Only then does the necessity for interdependency become unthreatening.   Only within that interdependency of different strengths, acknowledged and equal, can the power to seek new ways of being in the world generate, as well as the courage and sustenance to act where there are no charters. Within the interdependence of mutual (nondominant) difference lies that security which enables us to descend into the chaos of knowledge and return with true visions of our future, along with the concomitant power to effect those changes which can bring that future into being.   Difference is that raw and powerful connection from which our personal power is forged."

-Audre Lorde, excerpted from, "The Master's Tools Will Never Dismantle the Master's House," read by our friend, ally, anti-oppression colleague, Dr. Mary Smith Arnold. It was followed by a second Audre Lorde reading:

"The erotic is a measure between the beginnings of our sense of self and the chaos of our strongest feelings.   It is an internal sense of satisfaction to which, once we have experienced it, we know we can aspire. For having experienced the fullness of this depth of feeling and recognizing its power, in honor and self-respect, we can require no less of ourselves...The very word *erotic* comes from the Greek word eros, the personification of love in all its aspects--born of Chaos and personifying creative power and harmony...The erotic functions for me in several ways, and the first is in providing the power which comes from sharing deeply any pursuit with another person. The sharing of joy, whether physical, emotional, psychic, or intellectual, forms a bridge between the sharers which can be the basis for understanding much of what is not shared between them, and lessens the threat of their difference. Another important way in which the erotic connection functions is the open and fearless underlining of my capacity for joy. In the way my body stretches to music and opens into response, hearkening to its deepest rhythms, so every level upon which I sense also opens to the erotically satisfying experience, whether it is dancing, building a bookcase, writing a poem, examining an idea. That self-connection shared is a measure of the joy which I know myself to be capable of feeling, a reminder of my capacity for feeling. And that deep and irreplaceable knowledge of my capacity for joy comes to demand from all of my life that it be lived within the knowledge that such satisfaction is possible...

-Audre Lorde, excerpted from "Uses of the Erotic: The Erotic as Power," read by my doctoral sex therapy internship supervisor Dr. Victoria Codispoti.

The last reading was from Chinese poet Lu Yu, read by Lance's physical therapy co-worker Hsin-i Chang, with a final line that became the theme of our journey together during our ceremony and beyond:

The clouds above us join and separate,

The breeze in the courtyard leaves and returns.

Life is like that, so why not relax?

Who can stop us from celebrating?

After the readings, we sang a love-song duet that Lance had chosen from jazz singer Linda Eder, "And So Much More," accompanied by pianist Adolfo Santos, with lyrics by M. Yeston and music by F. Wildhorn:

"Count every raindrop in a thunderstorm

count every wave upon the shore

I love you just as much as that

and so much more

Take all the clouds that glide across the sky

and all the light within a moonbeam

and every bird that ever spread its wings to soar

how I love you as much as that

and so much more

Count all the days that there are yet to be

and all the ones that came before

you have as much of me as that

and so much more

Take every leaf that grows on every tree

and all the wishes in a daydream

and every note of every song we all adore

I'm there for you as much as that

and so much more

Now add the stars and planets out in space

and all the miles that keep them far apart

find how many--if there are any more ways

of counting things

let's start

How many seconds does forever have

how many creatures watch the sun rise

how many ways to say the words

I can't ignore

how I love you

as much as that

and so much more

as much as all that

and so much more"

Eder's song was reflected in the dedication we made for the ceremony: "Tzyy-Liang and Stuart dedicate this day to our families of origin and our family of choice who have provided us with love, courage, wisdom, and so much more." After the readings, I was the first to read the vows we co-wrote in English and then my best attempt at Mandarin with special characters and *pin-yin* pronunciations that Lance had made so that my tones were somewhat close to accurate:

"I, Stuart Farquharson Hayes, do take you Chen Tzyy-Liang, to be my life partner, hand-in-hand in sacred love, for our days together in this incarnation. I pledge to you with my unceasing love, caring, commitment, joy, warmth, appreciation, faith, and friendship. I ask all persons here today to support and affirm my vows. May Heavenly Father, Earth Mother, Great Spirit, Saints and Sages, the ancestors of generations, and all of our families and friends be my witnesses. Om. Peace. Amen. Blessed Be."

Next, Lance effortlessly spoke his vows in Mandarin and repeated them in English:

> "I, Chen Tzyy-Liang, do take you, Stuart Farquharson Hayes, to be my life partner, hand-in-hand in sacred love, for our days together in this incarnation. I pledge to you with my unceasing love, caring, commitment, joy, warmth, appreciation, faith, and friendship. I ask all persons here today to support and affirm my vows. May Heavenly Father, Earth Mother, Great Spirit, Saints and Sages, the ancestors of generations, and all of our families and friends be my witnesses. Om. Peace. Amen. Blessed Be."

Lance is a crier and he didn't disappoint in that department as he said his vows. At that point, pretty much the entire sanctuary was crying in unison--tears of joy and tears of empowerment on this day of singing, reciting, and dancing truth to power; we knew we didn't have legal marriage, but we were standing for love and, at the time, that was what mattered most.

Immediately following the vows, it was time to exchange the rings and place them on each other's ring fingers. We chose oversize metal rings with no gemstones; instead the extra-wide two-tone wedding ring composed of half rose gold and half platinum melded seamlessly together with a gentle undulating wave pattern representing commitment to uniting our diverse ethnic and racial family identities through time as one entity having begun our journeys 8,000 miles apart across the Pacific Ocean. Following the ring ceremony, we drank from the cups of bitterness and sweetness using the Middle Ages ritual that united same-gender couples in England discovered by gay historian John Boswell. Then it was time for the pronouncement by the Rev. Roger Jones of the husbands Chen-Hayes and an extra-long kiss by the grooms because who could stop us from celebrating?

We ended with a Unitarian hymn sung by all in attendance, "Love Will Guide Us," led by Second Unitarian minister Lynn Ungar:

Chorus:

Love will guide us, peace has tried us

Hope inside us will lead the way

On the road from greed to giving

Love will guide us through the dark night

If you cannot sing like angels

If you cannot speak before thousands

You can give from deep within you

You can change the world with your love

Ch.

You are like no other being

What you can give no other can give

To the future of our precious children

To the future of this world where we live

Ch.

Hear the song of peace within you.

Heed the song of peace in your heart

Spring's new beginnings shall lead to the harvest

Love will guide us on our way

Ch.

And with loud Taiwanese percussion music sounded, we held our bouquets high as we locked hands and danced our way down the aisle into our future, which at that moment meant the receiving line for guests. After the guardian angels and our guests danced down the aisle and through the receiving line, it was party time and folks were sweaty and hot (and that was before any dance music made its way into the reception). The back room opened into a large area for dim sum and the fabulous wedding cake with the interracial cake topper (because no one had cake toppers at that point with an Asian groom and a White groom together--double tops! -- we created our own with pictures from various past Pride parade events in our finest drag).

There was so much emotion that day evidencing the transformative power of that ritual in our lives and those who loved and cared for us most over the years. Seeing our family of origin and family of choice together united with us in love was something that neither of us had ever dreamed of as children or as young adults until we met each other. The ceremony was for us, but the wedding banquet for the wedding party the night before and the dim-sum and dance reception to follow were for our families of origin and family of choice.

We used to host an annual potluck party and our friends would cook up a storm from around the world. So, for our wedding we wanted food that was equally outstanding. We wanted traditional Taiwanese food (not easily found in Chicago in the late 1990s) and a really good cake. Friends and family of choice were most helpful in planning. Joe Mendoza designed the summer suits (although we forgave him for choosing a winter weight material as we were soaked by the end of the ceremony); Sharon Jackson, Whitney Bradshaw, and Shu-Min Lin did candid photographs; and our guardian angels (as opposed to best people) were Alison Hayes, Jim Coursey, Rahni Flowers, and Shu-Min Lin.

What the church lacked in parking and air conditioning, it made up for in moveable sanctuary seats that easily made way for the reception dance floor. We wanted to have the ceremony on LGBTQ Pride weekend and parking was difficult in that neighborhood on regular weekends and beyond impossible during Pride. So we figured if our guests only had to arrive and depart one venue for both the ceremony and the reception, that would keep festivities focused and parking drama at a minimum. We created a commitment ceremony with joy and fabulosity. We didn't want to call it a wedding at that time because of the lack of access to legal marriage and to challenge the sexist and property-based notions of marriage for centuries in most cultures. But we were in love and rwanted to celebrate our pair-bonding as partners-in-love, like other couples, and to have our relationship recognized by our families of origin and family of choice.

The wedding banquet featured the "sacred commitment ceremony" party and family members from out of town and out of the country, including Lance's niece Linda Hsiao, who was in high school in Buffalo, NY, and Lance's sixth brother, Chun Chen, who had flown in from Taiwan to represent Lance's family at the ceremony. My parents graciously picked up the tab for the wedding banquet. It was held at the best Taiwanese-owned restaurant in Chicago featuring pan-Chinese cuisine on the near south side in Chinatown Square. The reception's dim sum was catered by a good Cantonese restaurant on the North Side from the Argyle Street neighborhood where we often hung out on weekends with friends. A 12-item dim sum, while nowhere near a traditional 12-course wedding banquet, was a quick and fun way to have lunch in an informal setting prior to cutting the cake and dancing on the hottest afternoon of the summer.

We chose jasmine tea for the banquet and ethereal Elderflower for a toasting drink at the reception. The cake was our favorite part of the reception. We had become regular customers of the Swedish Bakery in Chicago, located in Andersonville northwest of our home in Uptown. Andersonville was the lesbian neighborhood in Chicago, and when we first met Lance had lived in BoysTown, the gay neighborhood, and our second condo was in Margate Park, equidistant between the two neighborhoods, which made us bisexual by location. The cake had four separate tiers of yellow cake filled with lemon cream and apricot cream layers covered in Lance's favorite beige marzipan with elegant white frosting embellishments.

The cake tiers were topped with fresh lavender, pink, and purple flowers that matched the rest of I-Li Hsiao's wedding floral designs.

Dr. Mary Smith Arnold was our mistress of ceremonies after dim sum had commenced as we cut the cake and offered each other size-queen portions for the first bite (but no cake-smashing). Mary, as a professor of Counselor Education specializing in couple and family counseling (and regular wedding reception officiant), commented that the gathering could tell how successful we would be communicating as a couple based on how well we cut the cake! We passed her couple final exam with ease! Next came the toasts from Lance's brother representing the Chen-Hsiao family, Alison representing the Hayes family, Rahni Flowers representing my friends, and I-Li Hsiao and Lillian Chen representing Lance's friends and co-workers. Alison welcomed Lance to the Hayes family and Chun (Brother #6) welcomed me to the Chen-Hsiao family. There was a lot of heart, humor, and fabulosity in the words used to describe our union as well as spontaneity and a willingness not to embarrass us, too much, during the toasts. Then it was time to toss the bouquets (we each carried one but no garters) and collectively returned to the sanctuary for dancing to music that Lance pre-mixed ahead of time (thank goodness for moveable chairs rather than pews) and like the rest of the ceremony and the reception, all taped by videographers. We later learned that the videographers had quite the time editing our sacred commitment ceremony and festivities; after we received the tape they shared that no other wedding tape had ever garnered so much interest and attention from their staff.

After the ceremony and reception were over, we conspired with Radical Faerie friends to celebrate with LGBTQ Chicago in style. Since it was gay pride weekend, the next day was the pride parade. We had seen a float with two gay men in white tuxedos promoting traditional marriage the prior year in the Pride Parade and it inspired us to drive in a different direction. We thought it lacked campiness, so we decided to have some fun knowing that we didn't have the legal rights to marriage at the time. It was time to flaunt our difference as gay "newly partnereds" during the parade.

Performance artist and international Bulgarian celebrity the Lovely KuLOVEly (a.k.a. Slava Pavlovna Bratislava) drove us sitting on the backseat ledge of a dark green Ford Mustang convertible with huge lavdender-backed painted sparkling banners on each side of the car that read "JUST MARY'D." We wowed the crowd in our purple and pink wigs and almost-matching, almost-white wedding gowns. Surrounding us were Radical Fairies in rainbow-color attire prancing down the streets. We were interviewed by a reporter from the Chicago Tribune after the parade, and our quotes appeared in the next day's paper. The reporter did a good job and stated that we had

had our wedding ceremony the day before and that there was nothing like dressing in drag to teach us—momentarily--about sexism and the realities of all too many women's lives.

I explained that I had been groped and harassed by a drunken man prior to the parade along the route. When someone (usually women) puts on a dress, bodies should not automatically be public property for men to harass (staight, gay, bi, queer, questioning, drunk or sober). It was the last thing we wanted to deal with during the "wedding" weekend. While the straight-acting crowd cringed at drag and leather, we thought it was important to celebrate the diversity of the gay community in the pride parade as a mixed-race, dual-national gay couple in full drag. After the parade, we fled the scene in style and escaped Chicago flying toward our *queermoon*, a.k.a., our gay honeymoon.

The traditional destinations and furnishings (heart-shaped beds at Niagara Falls or Las Vegas penthouse hotel suites) didn't do much for us. At the time, most venues for post-wedding plans had a heterosexual feel, so we had to do our research. I looked at an online gay travel site, Purple Roofs, which had begun to share gay-owned and LGBT vacation destinations around the globe. We wanted something in between Taiwan and the USA and thought that somewhere in the middle of the Pacific Ocean would be a good choice. The state of Hawaii was moving close to being the first in the country to declare marriage legal for same-gender couples (although it didn't happen until years later). We also didn't want to do the traditional touristy Waikiki beach in Honolulu. Our idea of fun was something with a gay flavor but more rugged with lots of flora and fauna. I stumbled onto Kalani Honua, the Kalani eco-resort. Run by a gay man (the always fabulous Gay Liberation Front activist and former professional dancer Richard Koob) and a board of directors, it celebrated traditional Hawaiian culture, wellness, the arts, and ecology right at the edge of the southern tip of the Big Island/Kehena beach near Pahoa, the largest gay community outside of Honolulu. Kalani was located in a lush section of vegetation in the eastern area of the Hawaiian Volcanoes National Park lands. I will never forget the smell of fresh air and Hawai'ian flowers when we arrived at the airport and across the Big Island as we drove with the windows down. The roads were rural and the vegetation was everywhere forming amazing arcs of trees overhead with fresh floral smells beckoning us forward. By day we could see the black lava freshly forming the newest earth on the planet and at night it was equally easy to see the warm red glow of the volcano and imagine the goddess Pele busy stirring up fresh new lava. Perched just off the oceanfront, we could hear the waves crash at night and watch the water glisten and head off for a swim either in the pool or down the road at the clothing-optional black sand beach. Kalani became our spiritual home. Richard Koob surprised us with a fabulous stay and we enjoyed adventures, activities, locally sourced pescetarian/vegetarian meals, a room full of drag, traditional Hula and other dance lessons, coped with mosquitoes (just like Taiwan), visited steam craters, lava tubes, beaches frequented by locals, and enjoyed the pool, massage, and the relaxing sounds and smells of rural Hawai'i. It was great to celebrate in a place that geographically created a mid-point between our origins. Little did we know the powerful effect that our first visit would have on our family. It was a necessary charging of our queer batteries for future legal challenges on the way to creating our family.

CHAPTER FIVE

DRAMA, DRAMA, DRAMA

NYC DOMESTIC PARTNERSHIP

Even though we had a great group of friends in Chicago and lived within an hour of my parents, and we both had decent jobs and a great place to live, my job was not a good fit. Lance helped me see that I needed to move on to new employment. Our first choice was the west coast. We both had offers but unfortunately in cities too distant from each other to make it happen. A commuter relationship had zero appeal. When I received an offer to teach school counseling at City University of New York's (CUNY) Lehman College, the only position we had looked at on the east coast, Lance agreed to return to New York City, a place he had found stressful and tiring, which was why he landed in Chicago originally. At the same time, Lance was struggling with a lack of creative outlets and not sure if he wished to continue a career in physical therapy.

Lance was interested in a possible career change to something more creative and both of us agreed that New York City had a stronger gay community, a vibrant Taiwanese community, and a more progressive political environment that what we had experienced in Chicago. For those factors, and that we had friends and family in metro New York City, we headed to the East coast in 1998 and quickly took advantage of CUNY's agreement with New York City that had been signed into law that Spring in which all city employees could enter into city-registered domestic partnership agreements with their significant others ensuring their partners and children health benefits. At the time, CUNY was one of very few universities that offered domestic partner health benefits to faculty and staff. But we laughed at the term domestic partners as it sounded like we'd be doing nothing but cooking, cleaning, and housework! Instead, we referred to ourselves with something more romantic: *domestic partners-in-love.*

After accepting the CUNY job offer, it was time to find a place to live, and in one weekend Lance received multiple job offers as a physical therapist and I went house hunting. I wasn't thrilled about living in the suburbs because of the less-than-happy experience I had growing up in suburban Chicago but Lance had only lived in large cities his entire life and wanted a yard. However, we couldn't afford anything in New York City with that description, so we compromised on New Rochelle, the seventh largest city in New York, which looked like a suburb but had a quasi-urban downtown. We bought a small four-bedroom house in a mixed-race neighborhood. It was more than what we needed at the time, but we were thinking ahead about future needs and didn't want to start too small and then have to move again.

We bought a 90-year-old Tudor-style home that was unoccupied for four years as the former owners had to completely renovate the house after faulty plumbing turned the house into an uninhabitable ice cube the winter they bought it. The location was just north of our jobs in the Bronx, 20 minutes in good traffic from the Taiwanese community in Queens, and 45 minutes, if lucky, to midtown and southern Manhattan, home to LGBT life in NYC. We were hardly the gay equivalent of Rob and Laura Petrie, who had moved out of New Rochelle long before we made our entrance. Although the home was 85% renovated, in the next few years we renovated whatever hadn't already been taken care of, including a water heater, a boiler (thanks to a scare of carbon monoxide poisoning one day caught by our detectors), and a disaster of a lawn including massive poison ivy from which I contracted temporary raspberry racial identity. We applied fashion police skills and created terrific gardens and the former ice-cube house with no yard came to life. We lived in what was once a working-class Jewish, Italian, and Irish neighborhood that was shifting to mostly African-American and Latinx folks. We had terrific neighbors including a few who identified as lesbian and gay.

The fall of 1998 saw our first political demonstration as a couple as we attended the political funeral for Matthew Shepherd. It was eerie marching and experiencing the kettling behavior by NYPD to keep us out of the streets but we were more enraged at the hate and heterosexism that surrounded his murder and the historic lack of justice for LGBTQ persons in the USA. But back in New Rochelle, even after one particular incident of hate, we still felt welcomed. As in Chicago, we had no qualms flying our rainbow flag in front of our home, especially during LGBTQ Pride Month. One day we returned home to find it had been stolen. Since we lived bordering a major East-West road in town, we figured it would be extra visible but it may have been a little too visible. We shared with our neighbors what had happened and a mixed-race family who lived near us were so outraged that they said they would start flying a rainbow flag and encouraged us to do so again. So, several of our closest neighbors all along the busy street did just that and no more rainbow flags ever disappeared. We had great allies. I also became involved in the fight for gender justice in New York joining Dr. Pauline Park on the board of New York Association for Gender Rights Advocacy (NYAGRA). We had several legislative and advocacy victories including NYC mayor Mayor Mike Bloomberg signing the first city transgender rights bill, which Pauline had written. On that day during the bill-signing ceremony, I asked him to hire more school counselors to support LGBTQ youth in NYC schools.

At the same time, Lance was on a green card since he had worked as a physical therapist during his graduate studies at New York University in the early 1990s. When we had the sacred commitment ceremony, we decided that I would change my name to Chen-Hayes first. This avoided any concerns about Lance being gay in his interviews with the Immigration and

Naturalization (a hateful name--we're all natural regardless of citizenship) Service (INS) for citizenship. While Lance cringed at having to be so careful about sharing his sexual orientation openly during an INS interview, he knew too well the history of hetrosexism, linguicism, and racism in immigration processing in the USA. The Asian Exclusion Acts in the 19th and 20th Century, the immigration ban on LGBTQ persons from 1965-1990, and the Clinton administration's advocacy and success in passing Defense of Marriage Act (DOMA) legislation legalizing state hate against LGBTQ marriages in 1996 were all fresh in his mind as he neared his chance to gain full citizenship in the USA. In early 2001, Lance had his final INS interview and was granted citizenship in the USA. He retained his Taiwanese citizenship as a dual national. He immediately applied to sponsor citizenship for his next eldest brother, Chun Chen, and sister-in-law Gloria Huang and their children Annie and Ray all living in Taipei. He had changed his English name legally to Lance T. Chen during the "naturalization" process (he didn't know how "alien" and "unnatural" he was before) and would become Chen-Hayes with another name change once he had the USA passport in hand. We celebrated another progressive voter in the house and the second official Chen-Hayes in early 2002. At the same time, Lance's career was shifting. He was tiring of physical therapy and yearned for something more creative. He chose to study graphic design at Westchester Community College. One of his instructors so loved his work that she taught class using his materials and hired him to join her graphic design firm.

Lance loved the work and won several awards, but the pay was poor. After 9/11, the bottom dropped out of the economy and the design world seemed to have less appeal. Lance had found a creative outlet but couldn't afford to continue to pay a mortgage. However, at this time, Lance knew that he was now ready to be a parent. He had come to terms with the challenges in his career and decided that it was now time to pursue having a child.

I was ready to parent earlier than Lance and according to my mom and sister I had been in training ever since I became a big brother at age three. I was secure in my job with CUNY and the house and neighborhood were fine. We spent a long time initially thinking about and exploring international adoption online and with friends who had pursued international adoption. We liked the idea of having one of us match our future child on at least one major cultural variable, most likely race, ethnicity, or gender. We also liked the idea of parenting a child of color or a mixed-race child. We thought that if we did international adoption, we would have a daughter of Chinese ethnicity and Asian racial identity due to the patriarchal Chinese culture favoring sons over daughters.

But right at this time was when China began to crack down on "single" parents who were actually same-gender couples seeking children in China, which made us sad and angry. We had no desire to go back in the closet, so that idea was dropped. At the same time, since we were living in a mixed-race neighborhood, we considered domestic adoption. As we monitored conservative forces around the USA and the legal status of gay adoption, we weren't convinced that adoption was the safest route for us legally as a family. We also wondered about "surprises" that might appear down the road of a physical, emotional, or legal nature.

So we next discussed the possibility of surrogacy to have more legal control over the process of creating a child whom we could parent from the start of life. Neither of us had felt a strong need to have biological progeny because there are so many children needing adoption or foster care in the USA and worldwide. But as we talked more with friends who had adopted and studied the literature, we became uncomfortable with surprises that lurked in the adoption process nationally and internationally. Having earlier ruled out international adoption and after evaluating the pros and cons of pursuing domestic adoption, we decided that pursuing surrogacy, although the most expensive of the options, was legally and emotionally the best route for us at that point in our lives in our early 40s.

The biggest challenge to us about surrogacy, however, was the cost—in the early 2000s the going rate, at a minimum, was $40,000 and that did not guarantee conception or a live birth. One of the firms we looked at, which was gay-owned and operated, quoted a starting figure of $80,000 with a fancy brochure that reminded us more of selling real estate than creating a baby. We loved the idea of supporting gay-owned businesses but that one had us priced out of consideration before we began the process. We also recognized that we didn't have cash anywhere near the lower estimate with both of us barely paying a mortgage that had our budget stretched to a maximum (we learned the hard way that owning in Chicago was cheap compared to metro NYC). We realized that we needed to sell the house after four years and move into something less expensive using part of the proceeds from the sale for the surrogacy.

The next big challenge was the legality of surrogacy contracts in New York State. Only four states outlawed surrogacy contracts at that time, and we were living in one of them—New York. We knew of folks who had gone around the law, but we figured it best to stay above board especially since I was a city employee as a CUNY faculty member and untenured. We knew that we either needed to move to Connecticut or New Jersey and we couldn't afford anything in Connecticut near our jobs. We chose New Jersey because it had excellent case law for same-gender adoptions and permitted surrogacy contracts. We focused our house hunt on Middlesex County, which had the largest population of Asians with many recent East and South Asian immigrants, bilingual families, Mandarin language schools, and Taiwanese/Chinese restaurants/groceries.

When we shared our reasoning with my parents about deciding to pursue surrogacy, they were supportive but didn't say much after our initial discussion. We found an excellent attorney (and at the time, the first in the USA specializing in surrogacy), Steve Litz, of Surrogate Mothers, Inc. Gay friends had a successful surrogacy through his agency and they recommended him with no reservations. After contacting him, we liked how he responded to our email queries, and we decided to visit him in person to see his list of surrogates and to finalize a surrogacy contract at his office in Indiana. After filling out extensive surrogacy paperwork in New Rochelle prior to meeting in person, we flew to Indianapolis and drove to the one-stoplight town of Monrovia, Indiana and met Steve. This was Lance's first and only time in the Hoosier state and he was unnerved at how rural the landscape was and at how White the state was with hardly any people of color to be seen during our weekend on our journey to finalize a surrogacy contract.

In Steve's office, we looked at pictures of potential surrogates and didn't find anyone we felt strongly about. There was one Asian Indian surrogate whom we both liked and if we went with her I would have been the sperm-donor dad. The rest of the potential surrogates were White and if we went with one of them, Lance would have been the sperm-donor father. We also reflected in our meeting with Steve Litz about what we wanted to say to our surrogate:

We desired a biological connection to our future child as the strongest way to support our family and that child's place in it legally and we liked the idea of open adoption as a part of the surrogacy process for the non-biological dad. We believed that our future child would benefit from adult honesty, clarity, and the ability to have direct and caring answers about everyone involved in their start in life. In addition, we wanted our future child to know the truth of their origins from conception forward. Every child deserves to know the truth about their origins and the uniqueness, courage, love, hope, selflessness, and kindness given by a surrogate that allows the pregnancy and birth to occur when two legal parents do not possess the genitalia that allows for pregnancy and birth using only our bodies in the process.

We wanted a healthy child but we could handle disabilities of all sorts if they happened in utero or after birth. We would, however, consider abortion in severe cases of genetic disorders or congenital deformities if diagnosed in utero as long as a surrogate was ok with that. We both had the skills to handle most developmental, learning, and emotional disabilities, and many physical disabilities, if needed. In seeing a surrogate, the qualities most important to us for a good match included her being in excellent health, having great wisdom and intelligence, and a commitment and comfort in helping create a mixed-race child for a mixed-race, dual-national gay couple. We had no gender preference for the child. If we had gone with adoption from China, our child would likely have been a girl and we didn't want to be exclusive in gender. We wanted to be surprised at birth by the child's gender and not know prior to birth. We would have been happy to parent any baby as we didn't believe in a gender binary, although we would be happy to raise a child who did. We had a lot to think about on the plane ride home from Indianapolis to New Rochelle with legal contract in hand to start the baby creation process. We could barely contain our excitement and wonder yet we didn't choose a surrogate at that time wanting to make sure we didn't rush a decision.

A few months after that, Lance and I were watching an episode of *Six Feet Under,* the cable television show that captivated us with gay-couple plot lines and the first TV mixed-race gay couple since its first season. We loved the treatment of gay characters and multiple ethnic and racial identities and family complexity in *Six Feet Under.* All of a sudden, the phone rang. My sister Alison said that she had heard from mom that we were interested in surrogacy and that she would like to offer to help create the child for us. I was in total shock. It was a little too ironic, however, that the *Six Feet Under* episode that we were watching was about a dead baby, so as stunned as I was when she called, I told Lance what she'd said and replied, "Wow, thanks, we can't believe it, and we'll call you back in an hour!" How could we say anything but a resounding YES to Alison's offer?

CHAPTER SIX

MAKING BABY WITH THREE

TWITCH

We had talked about potential family members when we first discussed surrogacy, but we ruled everyone out. We were not comfortable even broaching the question of asking a family member or friend to do that for us because it would put family members or friends in an awkward spot. We felt that we would be uncomfortable each time if the answer was no or if the answer was yes and then something unpleasant happened down the road. We agreed the best path would be someone whom we did not know prior to attempting surrogacy. What we gave up, however, was direct knowledge of the person's family history other than what they would be sharing with us, but we felt that outweighed potential damage to relationships between family members or friends. However, when Alison offered, we immediately agreed that there were no downsides whatsoever and that we should agree to her offer and proceed to explore the logistics.

Our excitement was limitless. We agreed with her rationale to engage in a surrogacy as a family member carrying a child for another family member unable to do so was ideal from a legal standpoint since we did not have legal gay marriage or any case law supportive of our becoming parents. She and her husband at the time had talked it through and while he was reluctant at first, they mutually concluded that they would help us within a few weeks of Alison's decision that she wanted to be our surrogate.

We had always had a good relationship with them (their wedding was announced just after we shared our gay engagement news and their wedding was a few months after ours in 1997). But this was a sibling gift a sibling like no other. Alison was an ideal surrogate in many ways. She had excellent boundaries. She was healthy and happy. She had no children and no interest in having her own child or in doing any parenting whatsoever. Aunt Alison would be plenty as a future role in the family. Alison stated that her primary reason for volunteering to be our surrogate was to put us in the best possible position legally and to save us tens of thousands of dollars. Plus, she would gain the health benefits from pregnancy if it was successful. But she was clear that this was a nine-month commitment (once pregnancy occurred) and that she would try becoming pregnant for 12 months but no longer. At age 38, and with a history of pregnancies on my side of the family all occurring to women in their mid-30s or early 40s since the 1950s, we figured it was worth a try. Alison wanted us to pay for her health insurance, vitamins, and all related medical costs. We readily agreed. We finalized the contract from Steve Litz with Alison as the surrogate. We accepted her stunning offer, which meant starting alternating monthly flights for Lance and Alison between central New Jersey, and Asheville, North Carolina beginning in the late summer of 2002.

If having my sister offer to help us create a baby was not enough family excitement, we had also made plans to sell our house in New Rochelle and cross the Hudson River to central New Jersey for a more affordable setting and one that welcomed surrogacy contracts. But for this move, we weren't by ourselves. Some years back, my parents had put out the call that they were ready to live closer to either me or my sister on the East Coast because of advancing age and my dad's health issues (dementia later diagnosed as Alzheimer's disease). A number of years before when we were job-searching on the West Coast, we had suggested to my parents the possibility of their moving in with us in the Bay Area.

To our surprise, my mom and dad agreed. But with no two job offers for us in the same West Coast metropolitan area, that idea fell through. However, with an imminent move to New Jersey, and knowing my parents had no interest in living in large cities, we asked my mom if she would consider buying a house together with us and have my parents live together with us under the same roof in central New Jersey as a soon-to-be three generation family. My mom was all for it, although she was concerned about moving her husband, living with dementia, half-way across the country. Lance and I continued house-hunting with my mom's two requirements: New construction and a first-floor master suite with few or no steps.

Of course, living in metropolitan New York City, where the cost of resale housing continued to climb, new construction without our budget was a big challenge. We found a community of new homes and large numbers of age-55+ adult developments. We looked at two neighborhoods for all ages and built a home at the best fit six blocks from turnpike exit 8A. In the fall of 2002, we moved to Merion Court in Monroe Township, with my parents joining us from Illinois a few months later after we had readied the house including Lance painting 3,100 square feet of new construction with creative designs to hopefully house three generations. Lance's mom also thought that our living with my parents was a great idea (and wished that one day we would do the same for Lance's parents).

Soon after the third baby-creation flight in November (and Lance's second trip to Asheville, NC in three months), Alison called with the news that she was pregnant. It was surreal. Everyone was thrilled. The excitement, anticipation, shock, and joy were palpable. But Lance, as a pediatric physical therapist, also cautioned me to remember that there can always be drama in any pregnancy and gave a long list of possible concerns to help counteract my exuberance and excitement. As word seeped out among friends and family the emails were fast and furious. Our lesbian friends elevated Alison to the status of major goddess and everyone wanted to meet her.

The next nine months flew faster than any time that we had been together as we stayed in regular email contact about how Alison and baby Chen-Hayes were doing, Lance returned to work as a physical therapist, and we adjusted to living in the same house with my parents. My mom's reaction to the surrogacy was couched in the sentence, "I always thought that if we had a grandchild, that Alison would be involved." Little did any of us know that my parents' only grandchild would have the genetics of her daughter, her son, and her gay son-in-law. Alison's commitment to the surrogacy process was something that my mom was proud of and she was as amazed and impressed with Alison's decision as anyone. Lance's mom and siblings were equally overjoyed and they agreed it would be wise to keep the news from Lance's dad in case he would react poorly.

The due date for the birth of our baby was August 7, 2003. Alison asked at the start of the pregnancy if we wanted to know the gender of the baby when the ultrasound was done. I was all for mystery; Lance could have gone either way, but Lance agreed on keeping it a secret. Although Alison accidentally found out the baby's gender when one too many ultrasound pictures were shared with her by her doctor, she kept that a secret from us throughout the pregnancy. We had no idea of the baby's gender nor that she knew until after the baby's birth. Alison sent us all the other ultrasound pictures (other than the one labeled boy parts) as soon as she could for us all to enjoy in person before our baby was born. Alison came up with a fun way to keep us guessing about the gender of the baby without our realizing it. Within a few months after she was pregnant she really felt the baby moving around in her womb. It was clear there was a dancer-in-training inside her because she was feeling regular kicks and other movement that made her twitch. *Twitch* became the baby's name until birth. Who says gay men are best at keeping secrets?

Lance and I acclimated to having my parents move in after 20-plus years of living separately from our parents. My mom was easy to live with. My dad's disease process, however, made him a challenge. We liked the large house and that my parents had the expansive master suite on the first floor and we had an upstairs loft, office, and two bedrooms—one of which we turned into a nursery, and we shared the rest of the common areas on the first floor. The ability to separate the generations in the house much of the time was an important tool for multi-generation living success. Mom had her hands full with dad and his care. We made sure she knew that we would only be calling on her in emergencies and that our plan was to do all the parenting for our future child. She was fine with that and happy to volunteer to help with whatever she could when needed.

While Alison was busy with Twitch, we talked regularly about our hopes and dreams for our baby-to-be and how we would parent. We agreed on a parenting style with ease: Being authoritative and democratic, as neither of us were interested in the dangers of authoritarian and permissive parenting styles, having had too much professional experience with children and families and seeing the dangers of both extremes up close in our professional lives. We also agreed that there would never be any violence used toward our child including no-spanking or hitting and no emotional or verbal abuse. We both had witnessed the damaging effects of violence in our personal and professional lives and agreed on our desire to model safe and effective parenting and relational skills for our child. Another area that we discussed was how to honor our child's multiple cultural identities. We wanted Twitch to grow up bilingual in English and Mandarin and we would start with English spoken by both parents. Lance would start to introduce Mandarin vocabulary words and we would look for a public-school system where Twitch could learn Mandarin. We decided to book Twitch and me, when the time was right, into local Mandarin classes at an area weekend language school.

We also hoped for extensive overseas travel in Taiwan, Scotland, and England over the years so that our child could be rooted in both sides of our family's ethnic and racial identities. We hoped to find teachers, role models, and caregivers of multiple cultural identities for Twitch when possible. Another parenting discussion was what would be the role of spirituality and religion in raising Twitch and how we would deal with family members of diverse religious and spiritual experiences and their varied paths. Both of us had difficult experiences with religion. However, we emerged from our experiences valuing spirituality. We wanted to ensure that Twitch was neither harmed by organized religion nor ignorant of the importance of spirituality in life. We agreed that Twitch should learn about the major religions without our imposing any one path. Our goal, instead, was to teach the importance of honoring the earth and developing spirituality through learning about social justice concepts and the importance of being kind and caring toward others through nonviolence. We wanted to give Twitch flexibility in developing a belief system about organized religion.

As a double-dad family, we also discussed how to handle heterosexism targeting our family. We agreed to seek resources for all of us whenever possible and that we would be out of the closet and open with everyone in all interactions as the research literature showed that children and adolescents whose same-gender parents are open about their sexual orientation contribute to a better outcome for their kids over time. We also realized that we could not always protect Twitch from potential hurt, anger, and sadness that can come from being teased about being different, particularly having two gay men as parents. At the same time, we vowed to equip Twitch with the skills to counter bullying or harassment or teasing head-on. We wanted to help Twitch learn how to value both human similarities and human differences as key to biological and social success for all beings on the planet.

We discussed how to be vocal and visible allies on the playground and in school to ensure Twitch would have love, support, and courage to challenge oppressions facing a mixed-race and hopefully bilingual child with two dads. I had made a DVD for Microtraining & Associates (now ProQuest) for professional counselors working with LGBTQ youth, and one of the scenarios was about an interracial gay couple leaving the city and moving to the suburbs and what they did when their 5-year-old was ready for school. Little did we know that years later our lives would parallel that vignette.

Another topic of curiosity among our friends and family was what Twitch would call each of us when born. That was easy. Because we wanted to honor English and Mandarin wherever possible, we decided on Baba Lance, as *baba* is father in Mandarin, and dad(dy) Stuart. Ba and Da (and Ma) are two of the earliest sounds babies make, and we liked the ability to both be called father in terms that each of our families had used when we were raised.

Also, we joined the national lesbian and gay-parent advocacy organization, Family Pride Coalition, and the local New Jersey chapter, Rainbow Families, to provide a place for Twitch to be around other kids raised by LGBTQ parents. Equally important for us as two dads were the support and resources available for us to share our journeys. LGBTQ-parented families share a commitment to celebrating the personal joys and navigating the legal struggles as same-gender parents in 50 US states and multiple countries with divergent laws affecting our families, relationships, marriage equality, and parenting/adoption/surrogacy rights.

Also, we talked about the types of toys we would use with Twitch. I grew up with lots of toys and Lance grew up with one; we agreed that toys were not that important--play was the crucial factor in children's learning, however--and too many plastic toys made big profits for toy companies and big messes in landfills. We agreed, instead, to buy children's books, puzzles, musical instruments, art supplies, sports equipment, and seek recycled materials over plastics. In addition, we would avoid gender-stereotyped toys (and clothing and diapers!) to allow Twitch freedom to grow up without gendering expectations early in life. Our plan was after Twitch's first year to limit toys and encourage folks to give educational or creative gifts or donate the money to children's organizations or libraries. We agreed to recycle/edit toys regularly and give away to other children so that gift-receiving would including giving # to others. We discussed other concerns for raising a child in the USA—obesity and the effects of corporate media on children and families.

We agreed to keep Twitch's diet as close to unprocessed foods and/or organics without being obsessive. We agreed no junk food, fast food, or candy (with dark chocolate and occasional desserts an exception). Since a main form of entertainment at that time for us was going out to eat, we wanted Twitch comfortable in restaurants and appreciating world cuisines. In addition to food, we agreed to limit Twitch's commercial exposure with no television (other than movies) and limited computer use with parental controls. But we wanted Twitch to see age-appropriate popular culture movies--another form of entertainment as a family. We agreed that Twitch would eventually use a computer and the internet with supervision to develop technology skills and use active forms of media (we didn't have our own cell phones at that point) and reduce commercials when possible.

One type of media that caused us a creative challenge in the planning process was a baby book. Where would we find one that reflected our unique family form? At the time, no one had created a baby book for lesbian- and gay-headed families. Lance had spent a lot of time trying to find one that made the fewest assumptions and incorrect labels regarding our family. The one he brought home was small but highly creative in its design and minimal in the terms it used to describe entries and family members. We only needed to cross out one "mom," lovingly replaced with "Aunt Alison," and we doubled the dad page to include baba. In our imagining process about our hopes and dreams for Twitch, we listed the following qualities that we hoped to instill in our future child and adolescent:

Proud of multiple ethnic, racial, and cultural identities

Bilingual or multilingual

Intelligent

Creative

Loving

Artistic

Well-traveled

Fun

Content

Kind

Friendly

Nurturing

Respectful

Courageous

Gentle

Just

Playful

Emotionally Present

Supportive

Loveable

Humorous

Happy

Helpful

Wise

Spiritual

Strong

Honest

Caring

Heartful

Real

Musical

Passionate

Accomplished

Meanwhile, Twitch was swimming, hopping, and dancing--constantly moving, bouncing, kicking and letting Alison know she was not alone. Alison loved being pregnant. She shared that almost all of her friends had nothing but drama during their pregnancies including horrible morning sickness. Alison had none. She enjoyed the bath of hormones and said that the nine-month period was one of the most pleasurable times of her life. She swam, did yoga, ate special vitamins, and gave up chocolate and beer. All of the health checks turned out fine throughout the pregnancy. In fact, Alison's doctor said that if Alison ever wanted to do this again that she had the perfect body for childbearing.

Alison appreciated the compliment but assured her doctor that this was a one-time event. She bought books on natural childbirth, attended childbirth classes together with her husband, and prepared for the big moment as best they could in their log home high atop a mountain near the Pisgah National Forest west of Asheville. By early August of 2003 we all were beyond excited and Alison was more than ready to go back to regular life and some beer and chocolate and take a big load off her feet, back, and stomach. The due date had come and gone and emails flew back and forth about the need to schedule a time to coax Twitch into the world because someone was having way too much fun staying in Aunt Alison's womb. But then the wonders of the high tides and the full moon's magic took over one evening, and soon Twitch was ready to encounter life on the outside.

Meanwhile, on the other side of the planet, Lance had alerted his mom fairly soon after Alison became pregnant that another member of the Chen-Hsiao extended family was on the way. She was beyond ecstatic. Her baby (Lance, the youngest of nine children) was en route to producing a surprise 16th grandchild and every week their telephone conversations were filled with excitement and the anticipation of yet another grandchild. In many ways, having a baby helped to strengthen Lance's relationship with his entire family and also strengthened the bond between our families as well because of the importance of carrying on the family name for the next generation, in the case of Lance's parents, for the sixteenth time.

According to Lance's mom, a Chinese psychic in Taiwan had many years ago predicted accurately the number of grandchildren she would have. Of course, it had been puzzlingly inaccurate until Lance announced the impending birth of Number 16. Even though she was over 8,000 miles away, Lance's mom cherished her weekly phone updates from him to learn the latest details about Alison's pregnancy. The bigger challenge for Lance's mom was when and how to tell her husband of one more grandchild in the offing without any fallout occurring for either Lance or his mom (déjà vu from Lance's parents' visit to our Chicago home).

Like his original coming out process, this discussion caused much consternation and planning between Lance and his mom. And like the decision-making process with his coming out story for his father, since his mom had done a great job of handling that story, Lance let his mom figure out the best time to tell his dad about the newest grandchild. When Lance's mom finally shared the news right after Twitch was born, Lance's dad was all smiles, equally excited about a new grandchild, and had just one question, "Why didn't you tell me sooner?" After eight years of planning, our journey to parenthood was an 11-hour drive away.

CHAPTER SEVEN

DADSRUS

FROM NORTH CAROLINA TO NEW JERSEY

That night at about 9:30 pm, Alison called to say that she thought she was going into labor. In the weeks leading up to Twitch's birth, I had been saying "baby baby baby baby baby." But at this moment the extrovert was speechless. I said, "Ok, here's Lance," and quickly handed off the phone, which shocked everyone and led to no amount of laughter afterward reflecting on how nervous most men (even extroverted gay ones) can be at word of impending birth.

We debated driving to Asheville at that moment, but my mom convinced us the 11-hour drive required sleep for the dads-to-be prior to embarking. But even though we tried, neither of us had a minute of sleep that night. The phone rang again around 4 a.m. This time it was Alison's husband (at the time) on the phone and he was at the hospital and Alison had just given birth to a baby boy (with extremely powerful vocal chords, according to Alison, and we could hear him clearly in the background). We grabbed a suitcase, jumped in the car and drove nonstop except for gas and made it to the Asheville hospital by 6 p.m. that evening to hold Twitch in our arms for the first time.

But there was some paperwork to attend to over the phone on the way that we had not considered in all of our planning. Nothing like being a mixed-race gay couple driving over the speed limit through conservative areas of Virginia on our way to meet Twitch for the first time now confronted with institutional racism in North Carolina! Aunt Alison's husband called and said that we needed to figure out what to put on the birth certificate about Twitch's race. There were only two choices in North Carolina: Black or White. So, the three of us discussed what we would do as he was half-White and half-Asian and there was no mixed-race box and no Asian box as we had erroneously assumed we could have both of his racial identities accurately stated on his birth certificate. We had discussed the pros and cons of creating a mixed-race child and how we would support his ethnic and racial identity development, but this was a detail that we had not considered. We later learned from an Asheville hospital employee that no one had ever heard of a baby born there who was Taiwanese. While we, as a family, all knew that Twitch was mixed-race, we would have preferred to list all three of his ethnicities--Taiwanese, Scottish, and English on the birth certificate to honor his cultural heritage as opposed to listing generic Asian and White racial identities. We assumed that the hospital staff would label him White.

Alison's labor lasted about four hours, and delivery was fast. Twitch shot out in less than 10 minutes. But in those 10 minutes, Alison let loose with exactly what she thought of us for the excruciating pain she was undergoing. Something only her husband should hear, we agreed. So there was our son, screaming at the top of his lungs and healthy as could be—and new Aunt

Alison was flabbergasted at how fast it had transpired and that all the training and goodies that they had brought along were barely needed. The total time in labor was about four hours and Alison said she made sounds that she'd never uttered before and never plans to make again. Delivery, Alison later recounted, was like a slingshot. Twitch made up for a week's delay by dancing into the world in record time once the moon provided the final momentum to make an overdue entrance.

The joy, pride, shock, and adrenaline melted into love at meeting Kalani Logan Kai-Le Chen-Hayes for the first time in the birthing room of the Asheville hospital. Even in his first day of birth, we could see clearly how all three of us were represented in his facial features. Aunt Alison said she couldn't get over how Kalani's hands and feet looked exactly like hers (high arches and all). *Kalani* is Hawai'ian for from the heavens/sky and from the Chiefs, *Logan* is a Scottish name on the maternal side of my family that means small cove or harbor. *Kai-Le* is the Mandarin name Lance created to mirror the sounds of Kalani's other two names using a K and an L sound. *Kai* is Mandarin for harmony and *Le* (pronounced Luh) is Happiness. We hoped he would have a harmonious happy life. We nicknamed him Kai-Kai.

Kalani's names represented his Taiwanese, English and Scottish ethnicities, multiple family languages, and his first name honored the state in the USA with the largest mixed-race population, Hawaii, and the earth-centered culture of traditional Hawaiians long before colonization. We honored our son's future experience as a "both-and" child with names honoring his multiple identities. What better way than acknowledging the powerful spirit, indigenous/earth-centered roots, and message of living in harmony and peace with nature and appreciating cultural diversity and the arts in our son's first name than the spirit of the Kalani eco-resort, site of our Queermoon and its earth-centered traditions?

We were overjoyed, exhausted, relieved, (but nowhere near as much as Aunt Alison) and ecstatic at good health all around. The sweetest moment in life for us as a couple was the first time we set eyes on Kalani. The full moon did its work to get our son moving out into the world that night. But he was not the only one—the hospital was full of women giving birth at the same time and had he been any later, Aunt Alison might not have had the birthing room she requested. We were also surprised (except Aunt Alison) that we had a son. Maybe it was our initial focus on international adoption from China and the likelihood that if that had happened that we would have had a daughter, and all of our friends guessed incorrectly that we would have a daughter.

We hadn't remembered in the moment that a higher percentage of births from surrogacy and/or in-vitro fertilization are males. But we knew we'd do fine with any gender and what was important was that Kalani and Aunt Alison were healthy. Some of our friends were curious why we weren't present in the delivery room, but Alison was clear that she only wanted her husband present and we were fine with that. Since she was giving this gift of life, it was her decision about how the pregnancy would start and finish.

We were dismayed, however, when the birth certificate arrived later and we were right: It listed only half of our son's racial identity, i.e., White, the racial identity of his birth aunt and me. It had no mention of ethnicity and completing ignored his Asian racial identity and Taiwanese ethnicity. Neither Aunt Alison nor I had been asked about our ethnicities (Scottish and English). The erroneous presumption of Whiteness, because his Aunt Alison was presumed White, was made by some hospital staff member. However, we also knew that as two dads living in New Jersey, disputing the accuracy of a mixed-race identity on the birth certificate would be a battle that we would not likely win.

Another glitch in the process of a legally accurate birth certificate for our two-father family was that in 2003 Lance could not be listed on the birth certificate in the hospital as the birth father because Aunt Alison was married. In conservative North Carolina, the birth mother's husband, if she is married, is automatically assumed as the father of the child. Kalani had to be legally declared by his birth Aunt that he was born "out of wedlock" (the smarmy phrase privileging one family form that sounds like a prison) in order to leave the father line blank on his original birth certificate. With all we had done to create this child, his presence on the planet was reduced on paper to an outdated legal term as "other" because North Carolina laws didn't recognize surrogacy or two gay dads (with a mixed-race Taiwanese/Scottish/English baby) as the legal equivalent of marriage. One other detail I noticed after we arrived at the hospital was that on all the other doors for babies who had been born, the Asheville hospital's women's auxiliary had placed a gender-stereotypical baby blue for boy or pink for baby girl tchotchke on the door of the room. But our son's hospital-room door, other than his name, was blank. Was it an oversight? Were they progressive and realized that this family situation was postmodern and beyond an either-or blue or pink memento (lavender would have worked!)? Did children born "out of wedlock" not get the tchotchke? Was it because Kalani's names were not easily read in terms of gender? The experiences of oppressive North Carolina laws and hospital traditions within the first 48 hours of Kalani's birth steeled us for future inequity challenges.

In addition, Aunt Alison had to sign an affidavit to declare that Lance was the father. This was how Lance's name was placed on the birth certificate as "the" father. Alison had agreed to terminate her parental rights to let me adopt our son so that Lance and I could be our son's legal parents. But the adoption process was not completed in New Jersey until nine months later. If nothing else changed our minds about the necessity of gay marriage needing to be available to all lesbian and gay couples who are pre-parenting or parenting, this process clinched it. If something had happened to Lance before I finalized my adoption process, Kalani would have been in legal limbo without a legal parent.

Aunt Alison recuperated before, during, and after our arrival. With a healthy Kalani in the care of Aunt Alison and the hospital staff for a second night, we went to our hotel to sleep and returned the next day to reunite permanently with Kalani staying in Asheville for two weeks prior to returning with the baby born in southern mountains to northern flatlands close to the Atlantic Ocean. Aunt Alison surprised us with an offer to pump breast milk for the first ten days and her husband transported it back between her home and our hotel. That week, we asked Aunt Alison to write in Kalani's baby book about her experience as Aunt Alison and why she chose to assist Baba Lance and Dad Stuart to create our family. She wrote:

"I knew that your dads really wanted a child for a long time, so when they said they were going to hire a surrogate I tend to be really practical and this just made so much sense to me. This way you would share genes with both of your dads, they would know the medical/family history of the mother, they could save the cost of paying a surrogate and use the money for raising you, and I could act as a legal safety net if anyone ever tried to take you from your dads. I got really excited at the thought of helping to bring you into the world so your dads could share their love with you."

"Uncle Jim and I talked over all the risks and benefits and decided that this was something we wanted to do. We had decided not to have children of our own for many reasons, but one of them was so that we would be able to make contributions to the world that we couldn't have time or energy for it we had kids of our own. Here was an opportunity to do just that. As Jim said, 'How many times during our lives do we get the chance to step up and do something that really matters, that's really fundamentally right, just, and kind?' We were thrilled to get to experience pregnancy, childbirth, and to become your aunt and uncle. I was 37 when you were conceived and 38 when you were born. Working from home as a part-time communication consultant, I was able to give my full attention to the pregnancy and enjoy the experience every step of the way."

We stayed in Asheville 10 days and began our journey as dads and baby in the beautiful Blue Ridge Mountains. In addition to enjoying the process of getting to know Kalani, we started to read out loud nightly, something that we agreed would be essential for cognitive and verbal development. Both of us were fans of the *Harry Potter* series, which I was in the midst of devouring. So, Kalani's first 10 days included nightly readings aloud of many passages from *Harry Potter and the Order of the Phoenix,* which J. K. Rowling had released a month prior.

On day three in Asheville, we decided as gay dads that it was time to go out for brunch, a meal that Kalani would get used to in our house. Kalani's second trip into the world beyond the hospital was to downtown Asheville's Early Girl Café. The irony of the restaurant's title was extra delicious (with our late boy having arrived a week beyond his due date). We had gone to celebrate our first meal out as a family not only because the owners were good friends with Aunt Alison, but they had some of the best farm-to-table locally sourced, organic food in town.   But perhaps the most fun was surprising one of the owners with who we were and how we were connected to her friend Alison. However, she didn't know the secret of who carried our son for us or why. She had no idea that WE were the reason Alison was pregnant. It was too tempting not to spill the tea and watch her reaction. She was speechless when we told her and could not believe that Alison had done that for us, and she was in awe. Something magical was in the air, however, as it turned out that exactly a year to the date from the birth of our son, she gave birth to their first child, also a boy.

A week later we drove home to central New Jersey (under the speed limit on this half of the journey with lots of stops) and Lance took four months off from work outside the home to care for Kalani as our resident pediatric physical therapist. We would have loved paid parental leave, but that was not an option from either of our employers at the time (my union, PSC-CUNY, fought hard for it as a benefit and eventually won it a few years later) and certainly not from USA government policies with few social safety nets for parents or children. I started a new semester of teaching at Lehman College as we adjusted to parenthood and Kalani adjusted to new surroundings in central New Jersey with parents and grandparents in the house. In those new surroundings, Grandma Lois and Grandpa Charlie had financed a matching crib and bureau for their one-and-only grandchild. Lance created a dragonfly motif for the room and hand-sewn curtains and rocking-chair pillows out of dragonfly-patterned material, and he hand-stenciled a dragonfly chair-rail around the room. He also gave a makeover to an antique rocking chair that was originally purchased by Kalani's great grandmother and grandfather Hazel and Curtis Hayes and would now calm and soothe the newest member of the family.

Also at this time, I was president of a national counseling group I had co-founded a few years before, Counselors for Social Justice. Lance did the web-design for the group, and this provided another outlet for shared activism. One of the organizations that we supported was Syracuse Cultural Workers, whose motto is "Art with Heart," and whose holiday cards and posters we have used since we met as their designs celebrate using creativity to challenge multiple oppressions with humor and artistry. We fell in love with their Alternative Alphabet Poster for Little and Big People, created by artist/designer Karen Kerney and designer Melinda Matzell, years before we had a child. The Alternative Alphabet Poster features the English alphabet with woodcut images surrounded by the names of 25 figures in social justice movements in the USA and around the world as part of the alphabet. It also included social justice and progressive terms to practice for each letter on the poster, including the terms gay and lesbian. It was rare in a country full of corporate media images for persons of nondominant identities to see images of ourselves and we wanted our son to see his identities, including his family with two dads, reflected not only in our daily living, but in media images whenever possible.

In addition, in the USA, with a conservative Republican head of the Department of Education head (Margaret Spellings) who railed against a 5-minute segment of the children's public television show that featured two-mom families and children, and a public broadcasting system that cowered and allowed stations not to carry the "offending" episode that had one eight-minute segment about two-mom families and their kids (Postcards from Buster), we decided that the Alternative Alphabet poster was an ideal antidote to fear and hate. It promoted equitable, peaceful, and inclusive family values. With bright pastel colors, we had it on our walls for years and made it an essential element of Kalani's childhood room.

Our activism continued in and out of the house as we transitioned to parenthood. We protested the build-up to the illegal Iraq war and had fashioned a large peace sign out of holiday lights that hung in Kalani's nursery window prior to his arrival and after to encourage the USA and our neighbors to promote peace instead of war. We attended our first anti-war protest as a family in Princeton on a night honoring the work of Cindy Sheehan. But even more important to us than protest outside our home was honoring the very special Taiwanese ritual done to honor Kalani's one-month birth.

CHAPTER EIGHT

THE MAN-YUE

It's a BOY!

Kalani Logan Kai-Le Chen-Hayes was born **August 13, 2003** at 3:49 in the morning weighing in at 7 pounds 9 ounces and 19.5 inches.

Kalani: Hawai'ian for from the heavens/sky

Logan: Scottish family name on Kalani's Daddy's side of the family meaning small cove or harbor

Kai-Le: Mandarin Chinese for Harmonious Music

The baby's Aunt Alison is recovering well and labor and delivery were quite fast! Kalani was born on the morning of a full moon.
We will be celebrating a one-month birthday party, a Chinese tradition, for all who are able to join us in honor of Kalani and also in honor of his extraordinary Aunt Alison (and Uncle Jim).

Saturday September 20, 2003, 1-3 pm

In Taiwanese culture, when a child is born, after 30 days a *man-yue* or one-month birthday celebration is held to introduce the baby to the world, friends, neighbors, and colleagues. Man-yue means one full (*man*) month (*yue*). Traditional foods are served including red-dyed eggs, sticky rice, and a one-month birthday cake. So, that's what we did. But we wanted to do something more than a party. We wanted to thank and surprise the guests of honor. How do you thank the couple, who gave nine months of their lives to give life to their special nephew Kalani? So, we flew in Aunt Alison and Uncle Jim from North Carolina and gave them a couple of surprises.

Since they love to travel we would send them on a couple of trips. The first trip was to Belgium, because Alison had given up beer and chocolate for nine months during the pregnancy and it was time to celebrate. The second was a chance to visit where Kalani's name comes from, the Big Island's Kalani eco-resort. Like us, they had had reservations about going to Hawaii due to its having a touristy reputation. But when they saw the website pictures and then toured both the Big Island and Maui, they saw pristine parts of Hawai'i and enjoyed a non-touristy side of the islands.

Yet, after all the euphoria and the celebrations were over, we had to deal with traditional questions lurking in our midst. Two Lehman College colleagues of my parents' generation both asked, "Who will stay home with the baby?"

We both had studied the literature on early childhood and child care options intensively as professionals. Our studies and experiences taught us that most of the world has had children raised by others at least part-time due to economics. However, we were dismayed at the tone of the inquiry, and the nonverbals about our plan to have our baby in daycare after only a few months. Clearly, they had been stay-at-home moms when their children were little and believed that was what we should be doing too (minus the mom part). But like most parents throughout history, most of us have had no choice but to work to pay the bills, and our family was no different.

While I had the option of unpaid paternity leave, it was nice in theory, but there was no way we could afford both of us out of work with a mortgage to pay in the New York City metropolitan area. Paid paternity leave, ironically available in most developed nations, would have been ideal, but it was not a reality in the USA in most companies and definitely not yet on the radar for either of our employers (although CUNY landed it years later). Lance returned to pediatric physical therapy in a home-care setting after we moved to New Jersey. He agreed to stay home the first four months after our baby was born, and after that Lance returned to full-time agency-based pediatric physical therapy work. We hired a live-out nanny when Lance returned to full-time work outside the home, and we thought that we had the perfect match in a nanny who spoke Mandarin.

Unfortunately, we were wrong. While her fluency in Mandarin was a plus, her child-care credentials never panned out officially. Since I worked most days from home he was available to listen and observe from the next room. While her skills were adequate, she had a difficult time with our gentle feedback on more than one occasion. After one incident related to some concerns and our attempts to give feedback to her for corrective action, she blew up in front of the baby and us. We decided to find alternative arrangements on the spot. However, we were faced, like so many families, with a childcare crisis. Lance interviewed seven different local pre-schools but only one of the seven had had any experience with same-gender parents. That was the one that we chose. We also liked that it was the only pre-school in New Jersey that had double accreditation in early childhood. The other deciding factors were the staff had unusual longevity in their positions in a field notorious for quick turnover and low pay, and the staff and children were of multiple ethnic, linguistic, and racial identities.

The only downside was its location was a half-hour commute out of our way in good traffic in one direction. However, we decided the distance was worth it for quality care with culturally affirming providers and a diverse set of kids and parents. When he was two, we switched Kalani into a linguistically and culturally diverse Montessori pre-school closer to home.

We both liked the uniqueness of the Montessori method, particularly commitments to allowing children to learn at their own pace in mixed-age settings; an emphasis on peace and caring in classrooms; and the life skills, practical life, and pre-Kindergarten creative play and learning activities. My schedule as a professor also gave me time most days to do drop off and most pickups.

We had wondered what it would be like being the only two-dad family in both of the pre-schools that our son was enrolled in. We found in both cases that staff and other parents were welcoming, friendly, and affirming of us and our family. Our families shared the same struggles around scheduling, pick-up and drop-off coordination, and all the details of making a successful daily transition from home to school. However, one issue that stood out for us in both schools was that we weren't sure that either one would have the resources to adequately affirm all of our son's multiple cultural identities or to affirm those identities with other children and families. I decided to research early childhood literature about multiple cultural identities for Kalani and to volunteer as a reader at both schools to share picture books with Kalani and his classmates regularly to affirm Kalani's multiple cultural identities and those of classmates and children who were not represented at pre-school.

This led to developing an extensive early-childhood picture-book library resource at home for Kalani's use and for sharing in school. We ensured culturally diverse and socially just themes were a part of Kalani's experience at home and in school as early as possible. We sought books that had colorful illustrations, that lacked stereotypical characters, and that reinforced themes of cultural diversity and promoting equity, fairness, and peace. We continued nightly reading to Kalani from books on our growing list of titles: Kalani and I read books in English and Lance and Kalani read nightly in Mandarin.

We also became interested in how more children could have access to early childhood literacy experiences, including culturally diverse readings. A colleague had been on the board of Jumpstart, the early childhood literacy group, and had informed us of their new project, Read for the Record, designed to raise funds and awareness for a college tutor program to help low-income children read regularly prior to starting Kindergarten, a way of closing achievement gaps prior to school starting.

As a family, we volunteered to assist, and did our small part to help set the Guinness Book of World record on the first Read for the Record day, which had over 170,000 people reading from one book on one day, *The Little Engine That Could*. I volunteered to read at Kalani's first pre-school, his Montessori school, and with neighbors on our front porch to assist in the record-breaking and to support early childhood literacy for all kids. We made that a family tradition as it honored ancestors on both sides of our family who were book-lovers and educators (both of Kalani's great grandmothers on my side of the family were elementary educators (one of whom was Michigan Librarian of the year), Kalani's grandmother Lois, a retired professor and librarian, and his grandfather, Charlie, a high school teacher and librarian. Lance's grandfather set up a school in the village for Lance's mother, Bi-Lan, to study.

We continued celebrating Kalani's first year on the planet with a series of celebrations and events, including first holidays and various milestones. The following summer included two favorite excursions. In June, we marched in the annual Gay Pride Parade in Manhattan, infamous for huge crowds and amazing sights and sounds. We drove into Manhattan, parked near Chinatown, hopped on the subway for Kalani's first train ride, and took our place in our first pride parade as gay dads. We had usually marched in NYC pride parade with Gay Asian and Pacific Islander Men of New York (GAPIMNY), and the GAPIMNY men were excited to have the first GAPIMNY baby via surrogacy (and his dad and baba) along for the parade. We snuck in half-way through the route as we knew none of us were up to the five-hour ordeal with an infant.

Lance created a logo for GAPIMNY that they had used in the parade featured on giant yellow balloons, so we were hard to miss as a contingent. But the best part of the parade was that the people of color contingent, including GAPIMNY, was first in line for the parade that year and we were the first dads with a baby to go past the crowd. Every child deserves to be welcomed in her or his first year on the planet by 800,000 screaming fans. It capped an amazing year. A month later, we traveled to Provincetown, MA, for Family Pride's annual Family Week. We had heard from friends that it was a surreal and enjoyable experience to be surrounded by only lesbian and gay-headed families for a week, and we enjoyed the experience.

Kalani was adored and adoring wherever we traveled. It was also fun to meet lots of other lesbian and gay parents and to compare notes during workshops, as well as to play together. We had our first dance with Kalani while we were there, and he hasn't stopped dancing since. Yet dancing with Kalani was a pleasure while we began to dance with the law again to secure our legal rights—which was a pain.

CHAPTER NINE

ALLIES & ANNOYANCES

ADOPTION & THE LAVENDER BIRTH CERTIFICATE

Ironically, had Alison given birth in New Jersey, we could have gone after a two-parent birth certificate immediately and a fast second-parent adoption for me. But Alison preferred to give birth in North Carolina and we agreed that it made much more sense for her to stay home. We also didn't realize how messy, slow, and arbitrary the adoption process was for second-parent adoption in New Jersey. An agency was assigned to us and a caseworker interviewed us in our Monroe Township, NJ home after we submitted the required paperwork and fees. It went smoothly but we resented that we had to do any of it in the first place and the amount of pages needed to complete the paperwork was excessive and time-consuming.

The caseworker was friendly and didn't ask any homophobic questions. But we hated that we had to do this in the first place since both of us were biological dads of Kalani, and we knew that this was classic heterosexual privilege with the law privileging traditional heterosexual family types. But the biggest challenge and greatest annoyance came when it was time for fingerprinting everyone in the house (other than Lance and Kalani).

My parents, since they lived with us, needed to be fingerprinted. My fingerprints and my mom's fingerprints cleared the first time, but that would never be the case for my dad. In fact, my dad went back a second and third time with no success, which was difficult for a man with multiple emotional and physical disabilities—just getting in and out of the house was an ordeal. The problem was, we later learned, that for many people in their later years, fingerprints wear away to where they are unrecognizable to fingerprinting equipment.

So after months of advocating with our lawyer, Bill Singer, the adoption agency, and calling the FBI (something I never dreamed I would do) to check on my dad's fingerprint status, the fingerprints became a constant headache. Eventually, after complaining to Bill Singer, who specialized in gay adoptions, about feeling like my dad would have to die in order for me to adopt Kalani, he suggested I write a letter to the County Surrogate (the irony of all titles) with that very query. After nine months of waiting to adopt Kalani, it was time for a little drama. I wrote that that my father would never have scannable fingerprints again due to his advanced age. I asked in the letter, "Would it take the death of my father, Kalani's biological grandfather, in order for me to adopt my own genetic son in New Jersey?"

The letter worked. Within a week, the fingerprint requirement for Kalani's grandfather was waived and we had a date scheduled with the judge to finalize the adoption. We later learned that this judge was one of the first in New Jersey and the first in Middlesex county to do same-gender adoptions. But we were angry about the delay and the entire process, particularly when it was due to inflexible rules about fingerprinting that didn't account for older persons' fingerprints wearing away over time (secrets Homeland Security no doubt wishes we would keep quiet). How could this delay protect our family? The process and the delays put our family in jeopardy because of an arbitrary time lag due to outdated family case law in New Jersey.

If something had happened to Lance or me during this time, what would have been Kalani's legal status? What would the legal status be for us if something happened abroad, as we planned a trip back to Taiwan when Kalani would be about four and a half months old to meet his Taiwanese relatives? Our family deserved equal protection in the eyes of the law from the birth of our child, as do all other LGBTQ families in states and countries where parenting rights are not guaranteed by law.

Even though the second-parent adoption was not final, that didn't stop us from journeying on Kalani's first trip to Taiwan from late December of 2003 to early January of 2004. Kalani was the perfect world traveler in the 26 hours it took door-to-door on the flight out and the 18 hours it took on the return trip. He slept in a bassinet most of the flight and was all smiles and sleep and didn't cry at all. Kalani kept the flight crew in our part of the plane entertained and mesmerized with his alertness and playful nature. The crew commented on how unusual it was for a child of that age to not cry on a plane, and we explained with only a little irony that as the grandson of a retired pilot (Grandpa Charley), that Kalani had flying in his genes.

However, as we attempted to leave the plane in Taiwan, one of the women passengers from our parents' generation asked, "Where is the baby's mother?" When Lance explained in Mandarin that Kalani had two dads, i.e., us, she was in shock and disapproved. But that didn't deter us. Once we were in Taichung, we barely saw Kalani for the next two weeks due to all the attention and love he received from his A-ma (grandmother), A-gong (grandfather), uncles, aunts, and cousins. But we often received curious looks and questions from strangers during the two weeks in the city of Taichung as two men of diverse racial identities with a baby in either a stroller or with Kalani safely strapped into a Baby Bjorn astride one of our chests.

Later, we had dinner early one evening at a Japanese restaurant near Kalani's grandparents' townhome in Taichung. We started explaining our story to the waitress, which we had done before in other places without incident. But at this restaurant, half the staff suddenly descended upon us. We could not get the staff to leave our table and stop talking and asking questions. They over-focused on us in a way that was uncomfortable for our family. We didn't count on a barrage of rapid-fire questions that prevented us from eating. While the staff were excited and fascinated by our story, we were hungry and less interested in being celebrities than eating good Japanese food.

Although movies have been made with titles like "Three men and a baby," they stereotype men as having no ability to be effective parents or they are a big joke about heterosexual men parenting together. Rare are the films that depict the lives of mixed-race or Asian LGBTQ couples and families, let alone those that have created families through surrogacy and adoption (2015's release of "Baby Steps" by Taiwanese-American filmmaker Barney Chung was a notable and welcome exception and we were script consultants). However, diapers and formula are easy, and most men have the cognitive and physical abilities to be successful at both. However, some folks in patriarchal cultures have a hard time conceptualizing that a mother does not have to be involved in raising a baby, child, or adolescent. Taiwan and the USA, while having progressive organizations, politicians, religious groups, and familes, have plenty of patriarchal reactionary elements as well.

For example, on the same trip, we visited the national botanical museum in Taichung and took a break to feed Kalani and Lance did the honors with the bottle. Out of nowhere, a woman who had been watching us came over and asked if Lance needed help feeding Kalani (without knowing, let alone asking, that he was a pediatric physical therapist with decades of experience with infants and toddlers). He assured her that everything was fine and that he didn't need her help. In a patriarchal society like Taiwan (and in the USA), some women have internalized sexism and often assume men don't have the time, interest or skills to nurture, let alone feed, a baby. We made a successful return to New Jersey and continued parenting Kalani despite others' worries. However, even with mundane tasks like shopping for groceries or gas, the next adventure lurked around the aisle across from the frozen food section.

We were in the Westfield, NJ Trader Joe's grocery store, and we watched an older White woman slowly passed by staring at Kalani in the grocery cart. She turned around, looked directly at Lance and asked, "Whose baby is THAT?" We replied in unison, "Ours!," and she quickly exited with a horrified look. We always liked Trader Joe's food, even if one customer in Westfield left a bad taste in our mouths. With the intersectional identities in our family, we wondered—was her comment due to no mom present, being mixed race, and/or something else? Doing our part to explode the hearts and minds of conservatives in the aisles of grocery stores--where they least expected it.

We never returned to Westfield and decided to shop at the Trader Joe's in Center City Philadelphia instead with more diverse families including LGBTQ people. However, the question would arise multiple times over the years as people made erroneous assumptions due to heterosexual privilege about two dads and a son. So, we've had to make decisions about how best to handle those questions including how to share our story in progressive media.

That same trip to Westfield, Kalani was starting to speak his first words and we stopped at a taqueria with great food and an attentive and friendly staff. Kalani, as usual, was entertaining the staff and everyone had a great time. When one staff member asked Kalani how the food was, in as loud a voice as he could muster, Kalani yelled with an ear-to-ear grin, "GARBAGE!" Maybe he was foreshadowing what our response should have been at Trader Joe's toward a certain shopper right before lunch!

A friend had put us in touch with Angeline Acain, the editor of New York City-based *Gay Parent* magazine, some years before we moved to New Jersey when we were in the planning stages of becoming parents. As an Asian American lesbian in a long-term mixed-race relationship with a child, she was interested in us and our story, and we thrilled to learn about her commitment to featuring LGBTQ familes of color and mixed-race families in her publication. At the time, she was the only one doing so across all English-language mediums worldwide. Angie would be the person most culturally adept and affirming at sharing the first news of Kalani's creation and birth. Several years passed and after Kalani's birth I contacted her. Angie sent the interview questions via email, I responded, and when the March/April 2004 edition arrived in the mail we were surprised to be the cover family with a picture taken by our friend Dr. Mei Chen, a professor of Counselor Education at Northeastern Illinois University, who was with her family in Taiwan during Kalani's first Taiwan adventure. We continued to correspond with Angie and she followed the first story with a June 2004 feature on LGBTQ weddings and commitment ceremonies that included our 1997 Sacred Commitment Ceremony. Once again, we opened the mail and discovered a second surprise--on her 2004 New York Gay Parent Guide we were again on the cover but this time in drag celebrating in our convertible the day after our ceremony in Chicago's pride parade..

But our time with *Gay Parent Magazine* limelight continued. We were excited when the property master for the *Six Feet Under* television show called Angie and asked specifically for a copy of *Gay Parent Magazine* with the three of us on the cover to use for an upcoming episode. *Six Feet Under* was the only TV show we both watched at the time. Unfortunately, the property master had a family emergency and the *Gay Parent Magazine* issue was never used, but we enjoyed our second connection with *Six Feet Under*, a real and provocative portrayal of a mixed-race gay male couple who became parents. It was the closest television image we had resembling our family's strengths and challenges in the media at that time.

We treasured our connection with Angie and her family and her commitments to LGBTQ families of color and mixed-race families and couples in a media landscape where we were usually ignored.

But slowly LGBTQ family media coverage began to increase in other outlets worldwide. We did interviews that became two different stories for the Chinese language press daily in the United States, *World Journal*, and we had pictures in those articles that included Kalani. We wanted to share our stories with Chinese readers and Taiwanese and Chinese communities in the USA but the writing quality varied. It taught us the importance of being able to tell our own story without the filters of others' cultural and media biases to assist others in seeing the strengths and challenges of being LGBTQ gay dads with diverse cultural identities.

One day, as I drove Kalani home from preschool in New Jersey, I stopped for gas and the attendant leaned over and asked out of the blue, "Is that your son?" Like a 6' 2" White guy with bleached blond hair driving a Toyota Prius with the license plate DADSRUS would be running around with someone else's kid with brown hair and half his facial features in his backseat fresh from preschool? "Yes, he's mine."

A Prius--not most folks' idea of a getaway car with a stolen kid because if you don't know how to drive it--you wouldn't get very far. I decided not to ask about the calculus employed by the gas station attendant at that moment, although I was tempted. Maybe next time I will shave my head and see what happens when I buy gas. Thank goodness Kalani wasn't having one of his three-year-old "moments." What might have been the outcome for a parent whose resemblance toward their child is questioned by others and the power they have to judge and challenge mixed-race and same-gender parents?

Then there was the weekly grocery shopping trip to the Farmer's Market, Wegmans, and a brief side-trip to our least favorite, Whole Paycheck (if you want to find gay dads in the 'burbs out on the weekends—grocery stores and gas stations!) for fair-trade chocolate and valentines. One of the store snack-peddlers asked, "You look like you're buying chocolate for your wife!" I responded by reaching for my wallet with a picture of our family and showed it to the guy (why wallet-size children's photos were created--for activist dads to shock unsuspecting capitalist employee silly assumptions) and said, "Yes, I am shopping for chocolate for my husband and our son." Although we didn't usually refer to ourselves as husbands at that time, borrowing the term in the moment was more delicious than the chocolate. We've had hundreds of encounters as gay dads where we've corrected folks assuming husband and wife to the reality of queer dads.

As we dealt with drama in New Jersey, we worked on more Taiwan travel plans. We visited Taiwan every other year with Kalani to strengthen his connections to Taiwanese family, friends, culture, and food. At 2.5 years old, Kalani and we returned for the Christmas holidays in December of 2005 and the new year's festivities in 2006. I played Santa for all of 15 of my nieces and nephews all around Taichung and gained great respect for Santa's time management skills and physique managing all those toys worldwide in one night. We ate favorite foods, enjoyed time with relatives, and did our first public lecture as a family in Taiwan at National Changhua University of Education (NCUE). A graduate student in counselling, Ta-Wei Wang, from NCUE, had contacted me after seeing an article about LGBT counselors and counselor educators raising children in *Counseling Today*, the newspaper of the American Counseling Association.

The article said that we would be in Taiwan for a family vacation. Ta-Wei asked if I would give a guest lecture. I responded I didn't know where Changhua was, and I wasn't sure if I had the time on a vacation. Lance told me Changhua was a small city southwest of Taichung, so I replied affirmatively that we would do the workshop together in English and Mandarin. We did a broad social justice issues workshop for counselors focused on affirming intersectional identities as we co-facilitated an Unlearning Oppression workshop, co-created by my mentor, Dr. Mary Smith Arnold, with Lance co-facilitating in Mandarin and Kalani made a brief appearance at the end.

We expected 40 participants and were stunned when we walked into the auditorium filled to capacity with 200+ undergraduates, master's students, doctoral students, and faculty from around Taiwan. It went well and the feedback was uniformly positive. Afterward, I asked about a sabbatical opportunity and professor of family counseling Dr. Sharon Shu-chu Chao, our host, agreed to see if she could get approval and funding for the following year. At the end of the workshop, Kalani appeared on stage with us and we answered questions about being mixed-race gay dads including Lance as Taiwan's first out gay dad, raising Kalani.

However, leaving Taiwan presented us with two issues of oppression. Attempting to leave the public area of Taipei's Chiang Kai-Shek Airport (now Taoyuan International) headed to the gates, a security officer, observing Lance's USA passport, asked why he had changed his to Chen-Hayes (which was incorrect, he *added* to his name). We weren't sure why he was asked that question, and we later wondered what the consequences would have been for various other answers. Lance replied, "It reflects all of my family," which garnered no response other than it was all right to proceed toward the gate. Then, when we reached USA customs in Seattle, Lance was asked by immigration officials to go off to the side even though Kalani and I had made it through the line with our USA passports. When we asked why, Lance was diverted to a different place, we were told, "You'll find out soon enough."

This made the earlier comment from the Taiwanese official seem miniscule. We sat for 30 minutes wondering why Lance, as a USA citizen traveling with a USA passport, (and a dual-national in Taiwan who used his Taiwanese passport in and out of Taiwan) would be asked to step aside — was it be being bilingual, Asian, gay, with a partner and child, being a recent US immigrant, or some combination? We would never know. Within half an hour, Lance's name was called and he was told he was free to go. but no reason was given as to why he was stopped. We wonder every time we go through customs, how will we be treated? Although some countries recognize our relationship and our family status, traveling across USA state borders, let alone national boundaries, can bring major challenges to our status as a couple and as a family especially in times of emergency or need for hospital care. We have no choice but to remain vigilant, however, it doesn't deter us.

An example in state legal variations in the USA was that when Kalani was born in North Carolina, he had only Lance on the birth certificate. It was ironic since Lance is Asian yet Kalani's birth certificate inaccurately lists a mixed-race child as White. However, we were thrilled one day when our lawyer, Bill Singer, called and said that he had found a lesbian lawyer through a Lavender Law group connection who had success putting two moms from out of state on their baby's birth certificate in North Carolina. In that case, like ours, at least one or both of the moms had out-of-state residency. Due to the full faith and credit law of the USA *Constitution*, North Carolina was legally required to follow the law from the moms' home state--both had to be on the birth certificate and the state of North Carolina legally had to honor home state laws. We were excited to learn about this potential for amending the original birth certificate and we encouraged Bill and the North Carolina-based lesbian lawyer to pursue leads on Kalani's behalf.

Eventually, the North Carolina lawyer moved the process along successfully. Once the application for amending the birth certificate was submitted, the North Carolina birth certificate division contacted me and explained who they were. They asked for my original name when I was born. At the time, I could not figure out why they wanted that information. However, if that detail was what they needed, I had nothing to lose. We also learned that quite a behind-the-scenes political stink occurred when conservative elements in state government learned about our request, one that would have been denied had we been North Carolina residents.

Eventually, Bill called with news we never imagined. The amended birth certificate was in his office in New Jersey. We were overjoyed at what was a legal first for gay dads with a child born in North Carolina. We were the first male couple granted a North Carolina amended birth certificate with two men listed as parents. However, our lawyer shared that there was a detail he needed to explain. North Carolina used the same birth certificate form for us as all other couples without changing any of the blanks. So, with my "maiden" birth name, I was listed on the line for mother. Now we knew why I needed to give my original name when Kalani was born. We laughed about it and shared with Bill that it was ok with us, because one look at me and everyone would know I am no mom nontwithstanding a few moments in drag over the years.

At about that time, my mom had sent some information to her college alumnae association about who she was living with (us and her husband) and the editor contactd her and said that they were doing an issue on the changing family. The editor was curious if mom and the rest of the family would be interviewed or photographed for the story. We talked about the pros and cons of appearing in the publication, and we agreed that my mom's alma mater had a progressive reputation and would feature our family in a culturally affirming light. We were not disappointed.

They hired photographer Ricardo Barros, who came to our home and did a photo shoot of three generations of our family at play. Kalani was understandably reluctant at first, but the photographer helped him warm up for a humorous picture featuring a unique twist on "family ties" that echoed the movie "Home Alone." The story, the graphics, and the photos illustrated multiple households, a variety of non-traditional family types, several lesbian and gay-headed families, and some mixed-race families in depth. We were excited when the issue arrived that we had been selected as the cover family for that edition of the *Mt. Holyoke* Alumnae Association magazine: https://issuu.com/mhcalumnae/docs/2006_summer_1.1

In our wildest dreams as children, adolescents and young adults, neither of us imagined being on the covers of national publications, let alone as out gay dads. While both of us had contemplated marriage to women, that would have been a disaster for everyone involved. I remember assuming that I would never be partnered long-term, let alone married, and I didn't even think about kids until my early 30s because it was not part of how I saw my life or the lives of any bisexual or gay people I knew. Similarly, Lance loved kids, but assumed in his career that he would work with other people's children for a lifetime with no plans on starting his own family. But now that we were parents, we wanted to immerse Kalani in his bicultural and bilingual identities at home and abroad in the USA and Taiwan.

CHAPTER TEN

MANDARIN IMMERSION

TAIWAN SABBATICAL

What were we thinking going on sabbatical for 6 months with a tempestuous three-year-old 8,000 miles from home? The top reason was to give Kalani the chance to spend six months with Taiwanese family members and immerse in Mandarin language and Taiwanese culture. We found a Montessori school in Taichung that taught a curriculum focused on traditional Taiwanese culture and the environment in Mandarin and Kalani adjusted instantly as the new teacher held his hand for the first meeting and we watched her care and love toward Kalani as he began his Mandarin immersion. Kalani developed basic fluency in Mandarin, a larger Mandarin vocabulary, and the ability to speak in small sentences at school and at home.

We wanted Kalani to be in as similar an environment as possible from the school we left in New Jersey other than the language of instruction (and the weather). The principal, teachers, and other parents were usually affirming of our family configuration (although not all families knew about the uniqueness of our family). We were happy and relieved at how easily Kalani transitioned into the school and how quickly he learned Mandarin with 8 hours a day of exposure at school and constant exposure at home.

Two caveats about the school were related to forms and celebrating Mother's day. When the children were given the chance to go on a field trip to a doctor's office for health examinations, one of the teachers gave Lance the official government forms for student health examinations and he filled them out returning them with the Chinese character for parent marked over where the traditional "father" and "mother" were listed.

When Lance gave the forms to the lead teacher and shared that the documents needed to be inclusive when listing parents and family types, the teacher responded that the forms represented the "average heart," meaning they did not want to challenge the "normative" family type in Taiwan. Ironically, our home Montessori school in New Jersey had used application forms with exclusive language about family type and parent names and we encouraged them to change their forms with no success so so we changed schools in New Jersey after that.

The second issue in Taiwan, however, was that the Taichung Montessori school staff were surprised that we were not participating in a weekend fundraiser celebrating Mother's Day. Although we had alerted teachers that Kalani celebrated his grandmothers on Mother's Day and would be welcome to participate in all activities to honor his grandmothers, the staff did not understand the dilemma our family faced with that holiday. So, we solved the situation, in addition to discussing his Aunt Alison with Kalani and with his teachers, by sharing with Kalani that he has two dads and a special "mom." For Kalani, "mom" is Mother Earth and he can celebrate her anytime including Mother's Day.

Speaking of mom, Lance's mom was beyond excited counting the days until we arrived in Taichung for our sabbatical. She was overjoyed that "her baby," her special son-in-law, and her baby's baby (Kalani) would spend six months in her townhome. She looked forward to our presence and we loved her doting and attention while we stayed with her. In addition, Kalani was excited to spend time with his *A-ma* and *A-gong* and all of his uncles, aunts, and cousins. Kalani bonded instantly with almost everyone in the family and spent hours entertaining everyone with songs, dances, stories, and creative play. We were amazed at Kalani's willingness to try new foods, because he was a pretty picky eater prior to arrival in Taiwan. Kalani had always liked a few types of seafood, but overnight he learned to eat whole fish, including fish heads (thanks to Chun, brother #6!), fishtails, and eyeballs, something that, unless you are from an island nation or seafood culture, is rare for a 3-year-old. Then there was the chance to watch family members playing *Mah-jongg*, which both Kalani and I enjoyed observing.

In addition, Kalani and I had the chance to spend extended time learning about Taiwanese holidays and traditions. We both enjoyed being in Taiwan for Lunar New Year and enjoyed the chance to be in a country where real fireworks are legal and erupted nonstop during the holidays. Kalani initially had some fears about firecracker noise after we went to an Autumn Moon festival in Philadelphia where real firecrackers were used. We weren't sure how Kalani would react in Taiwan with firecrackers going off at all hours of the day and night, but he grew to enjoy the sounds and sights. The Lunar New Year food and festivities, including lots of lion dancers, were better than we had expected. Kalani's family and school made elaborate preparations including all the traditional foods. But the best part of the Lunar New Year festival was the distribution of *hong bau,* red packets filled with money from elder members of the family to younger family members.

Kalani knew all about the ritual, and in the USA, he had been the recipient of one or two *hong bau* annually. But with all the relatives gathered at home in Taiwan, and with Kalani being the youngest relative, he received a small avalanche of *hong bau* and designated himself a happy *hong bau* elf. At the end of the Lunar New Year festival, we had the chance to attend the Lantern Festival and enjoy the glowing artwork of handmade lanterns in Taichung and Taipei. Ironically, Lance did some freelance (no pun intended) translation for the City of Taipei for the written advertising copy about the festival lanterns on display, so we all had an early introduction to the festivities from home.

Another holiday festival new for Kalani and me was the tomb-sweeping holiday honoring the ancestors. A bunch of family gathered and went to the family graveyard, which our family calls the Hsiao-Chen garden, on a mountainside overlooking the city of Taichung. The design of the gravesite is a mix of traditional and modern, and includes a unique set of sculptured hands in prayer lifting up toward the sky designed by Lance's brother #3, an architect. Kalani usually liked to clean up at home and at school, and he was happy to take a cleaning cloth and clean each of the tombstones without prompting from any adults. The Hsiao-Chen garden has plots for Kalani's great grandparents, grandparents, the seven brothers and their significant others (including baba and dad), and their children and grandchildren. We explained to Kalani the significance of the family graveyard and he enjoyed the day, including performing bows to the ancestors.

The next reason for sabbatical was time for Lance to spend with his family and assist his father, who had a series of health setbacks. Another reason was to give me a first sabbatical as a professor and time for extended writing. I attempted a sabbatical a few years before from CUNY, but I applied for a 100% paid one, a rarity in that system. We could not afford to take a pay cut at that time. I was not approved for the full-pay sabbatical, and in 2006 I applied again for a half-year sabbatical at 50% pay. Being in a union (Professional Staff Congress or PSC-CUNY) paid off. The sabbatical was approved, and with a new contact, the pay rate became 80% just in time for our departure, still not easy on our budget, but better than the prior 50% pay rate. Lance gave up his salary for the 5.5 months in Taiwan, so finances were tricky balancing a mortgage and other expenses in the USA and a Taiwan National Science foundation grant that paid a small salary for teaching classes at National Changhua University of Education (NCUE).

Living with Lance's parents in their large townhouse in central Taichung kept expenses minimal along with a car borrowed from Lance's brother #1. The sabbatical's main purpose for NCUE was for Lance and I to co-teach one bilingual section of master's students and I taught one section of doctoral students in sexuality counselling in English, the first time sexuality counseling was taught in a graduate counseling program in Taiwan, let alone by a gay couple.

Lance also received multiple referrals for private physical therapy clients, consultations, and invitations to lecture and present seminars for his sabbatical. The students and faculty member who facilitated my sabbatical, Dr. Shu-chu (Sharon) Chao, encouraged us to write our couple and family memoir for both English and Chinese-language audiences as part of the sabbatical.

In addition, we enjoyed traveling around Taiwan on the weekends and made multiple trips to Taipei, including Taipei 101, at the time, the world's tallest building, which combined both traditional and modern Chinese architectural elements, great restaurants, and we spent time with Chun, Lance's brother #6, and family. We visited the Beitou hot springs, site of Taiwan's early movie industry, and Danshuei, the western edge of Taipei County at the confluence of the Danshuei River and the Taiwan Straits. Since our last visit in the 1990s, a huge fishing wharf was constructed and we enjoyed the scenery and traditional foods. The festival atmosphere near the waterfront (including Taiwan's first gay beach) was reminiscent of both San Francisco and Provincetown, Massachusetts.

Other journeys took us to the historic sites and temples in LuGang, the original port city of Taiwan, and to sites and temples throughout Taichung and Tainan and the fresh coastal air, mountains, and Pacific Ocean scenery of the eastern coastal town of Hualien and surroundings. We enjoyed traditional architecture and traditional food and dessert and the local scenery. Our only regret was that we did not have more time to tour Taiwan's southeastern coast, but we saved that trip for a future journey when Kalani was older.

We also managed a long weekend in Hong Kong to see long-time friends Andrew Mak and Winston Lin who had lived in NYC for years but had returned to Hong Kong, and we toured the sight and sounds of Hong Kong Disney with perhaps the only 3-year-old on the planet who didn't yet know who Mickey Mouse was. The biggest gift of the Hong Kong trip was three days of pollution-free clear skies.

In both Taiwan and Hong Kong, we found a more visible lesbian and gay presence than our past visits, although Taiwan took the lead of the two — nations—no surprise considering the democratic reforms Taiwan underwent in the 90s and continues to model for the rest of Asia. During our stay in Taiwan, we attended a lesbian moms and "wannabe" moms gathering (the forerunner of the Taiwan LGBT Family Rights Advocacy Association) to share our story as a Taiwanese-American rainbow family. We learned about the strengths and difficulties (including a law banning the use of reproductive technologies outside of marriage) facing LGBTQ people in Taiwan attempting to become parents and contributed an annotated bibliography of English-language children's picture books with LGBTQ-headed families for their website, something that no one had any access to in Mandarin, Taiwanese or indigenous languages at that time. Many of the women at the gathering felt the need to remain closeted while raising their children, yet they organized groups like this earlier than gay men in Taiwan. At the same time, we were glad to present as an out gay couple and talk about the emotional benefits for Kalani with our being out as gay dads and what the potential dangers are for children whose parents remain closeted.

We suggested a possible compromise for LGBTQ parents to be open with their children and then help them manage their parents' and family identities indirectly outside the home versus directly inside the home.

We learned that the Tongzhi Hotline Association, the primary LGBTQ rights group in Taiwan, had developed groups for parents of LGBTQ people to meet in major Taiwan cities, and that LGBTQ youth groups had a begun in Taiwan. This was exciting and an important development in Taiwan's LGBTQ community: 1.) to create allies among heterosexual family members and friends, 2.) to enlarge political support for LGBTQ singles, couples, and same-gender-parented families in legislation, and 3.) to support LGBTQ youth coming out in schools and families.

We also hoped for Taiwan-wide change as Taipei city allowed foster parenting for gay and lesbian parents. Many of the lesbian moms and wanna-be moms we spoke with were empowered by our being out as gay parents and agreed it was important for couples who have the ability to be do so to be out of the closet in Taiwan and elsewhere in Asia to pave the way for others.

This demonstrated the political progress that LGBTQ individuals, couples and families have made in Taiwan since martial law was lifted in the 1990s. At the same time, being out of the closet for Taiwanese remained a challenge, particularly for gay men who lose some male and traditional family privilege when they exit the closet.

On a humorous note, one night after a show, Lance accidentally booked the three of us into a nearby *love motel,* which made us howl once we realized what the accommodations were best known for. While love motels exist around the globe in many nations, with Taiwanese families living in very close quarters with multiple generations, there isn't always a lot of time or space at home for privacy. Love motels play an important function for ensuring uninterrupted couple time. Love motels also serve as places for sex work (like barbershops and some KTV palaces/karaoke bars in Taiwan—more things I learned on sabbatical).

Toward the end of sabbatical, we celebrated our 10-year anniversary from the date of our Chicago sacred commitment ceremony (June 28) in Taichung. Ironically, since we were returning to the USA in a few days, we had barely remembered and quickly decided on a restaurant (and lacked child care so Kalani joined us). At the restaurant, the food was good, but we laughed when one of the servers, a middle-aged woman, asked about where Kalani's mom was and when we told her the story, she was in disbelief. Fortunately, the food was excellent. She must have shared the news with another server, because he kept coming over to flirt with Lance (and that took quite a bit of courage in a conservative society with both me and our son at the table—and probably had no clue how good Kalani's

Mandarin was). As we left the restaurant, the server ran to the door to call out greetings and goodbye to Lance. We could barely walk we were laughing so hard.

The real anniversary present was a total surprise and came earlier that day. We received a memento book prepared by the NCUE master's degree sexuality counseling cstudents whom we had taught all semester. They prepared multiple pictures and testimonials about their experiences with us in class each week and how moved they were by our presence teaching about sexuality counselling and how we lived and loved as an out gay couple with a child. Each entry had an English side and a Mandarin side. Their great appreciation for learning, their trust in us, and their openness, honesty, and growth during our time together was humbling and a highlight of our time in Taiwan. But unbeknownst to them, they gave the memento book to us on the last day of class, which was June 28th, the tenth anniversary of our Sacred Commitment Ceremony.

While in Taiwan, I was on the U.S. State Department website looking at the requirements for dual nationals. When we learned that dual citizenship was legal, Lance renewed his Taiwanese passport and became a dual national while we were in Taiwan. The next step was to find a way for Kalani to become a dual national, but we needed both the original and the amended birth certificates, and we only had the amended one with us in Taiwan. But that would have to wait until the next chapter in Lance's life. Upon our return to the United States after sabbatical, Lance realized that he wanted to pursue a lifelong dream of a doctoral degree. Lance enrolled in an online doctoral program in physical therapy while working full-time and parenting. In the summer of 2010 he graduated with his doctorate. Lance didn't have time to focuse on the complex process of going after Kalani's dual national status until after he graduated. However, when we approached the subject after his graduation, it was not clear whether Kalani would have more opportunities as an international student in Taiwan if he chose to attend college there so we decided against Taiwanese citizenship only to revisit it as politics in the USA shifted years later. And speaking of opportunities, as parents, we were ready for some reconnection with other gay men--diapers and baby clothes only go so far in a gay relationship before it's time to get with the guys for adult time out.

CHAPTER ELEVEN

DADS' NIGHT OUT

Like other new parents, we had an idea but no lived experience of the shifts that having a child brings to life for a couple emotionally, socially, and physically. We both had colleagues who repeatedly said, with a smile on their faces, "Your lives really are going to change," and "Life will be so different after having a child," but we didn't know what they meant until well into the middle of bottles, , burping, and sleep deprivation.

As gay men, we realized that, like heterosexuals with children, once you have children, social lives with single friends are harder to maintain, and couple socializing is often limited to parents with children centered around kids' birthday parties and school events. We didn't have a lot of gay and lesbian couple friends with children nearby, and that was a challenge as a dual-career couple other than our annual summer dinner party, when lots of folks flocked to see us from the city. But other than that party, we had to travel away when we could to arrange a LGBTQ+ family-friendly outing, which was with a toddler.

We lived as a 3-generation family together first in Monroe Township and then on Sullivan St. in Plainsboro, NJ, an area with a large East Asian, a larger South Asian population, and a diminishing White population with multiple Asian languages spoken. But greater Princeton wasn't home to a lot of gay people, particularly those who unaffiliated with the university.

So, after a few years in central New Jersey as gay dads whose entertainment consisted of restaurants, movies, the gym, and occasional gatherings with local friends, we sought a social and political outlet as gay men. We, (a.k.a. "the diversity divas"), needed to be more than dads at least once a week for fun and support as a gay couple. We were a happier couple if we had weekly time away from parenting responsibilities. Since the New Jersey Gay Men's Chorus (NJGMC) practiced weekly on Monday nights in Princeton, one night a week out worked in our over-scheduled lives. The auditions were painless, and we enjoyed singing with them for years.

The chorus had excellent musicality and the pieces were in various languages. The music challenged us, however, to find more time to practice to ensure our parts are in good shape for concerts. Lance had sung extensively as a child, adolescent and young adult, while I performed instrumental music (oboe, alto sax, and piano) throughout elementary, middle, and high school. I had sung through middle school but was embarrassed that I could still sing soprano in my freshman year of high school. Due to internalized heterosexism, I stopped singing for fear of being targeted as gay due to my voice having not changed by that time. NJGMC provided a safe and healing atmosphere to let the inner diva out once again. NJGMC revived our passion for singing, performing and all the more fun in the company of other gay men. A highlight was performing one night at Carnegie Hall.

The chorus members were supportive of us as dads, if not a little surprised since most of the men were not parents. We were welcomed as a family and at every break our brothers inquired about how "the baby was doing."

We started to do some gigs with the chorus, smaller concerts around the state, as our schedules permitted. This helped publicize the chorus, and it gave us the chance to perform as a smaller ensemble, including the NJ gay pride parade. The fashion police in us enjoyed the chance to buy our first tuxedos for concerts (Lance, I can't find my cufflinks!). We gathered a group of friends together from NYC and NJ and usually had dinner prior to the concerts twice a year for our shared love of music and politics. Singing in a gay chorus allowed us to do both at the same time. Kalani occasionally went to rehearsals transfixed at the sights and sounds (and sang with us when we marched together in the NJ gay pride parade in Asbury Park).

As we developed a musical social outlet for us, we also focused on Kalani's musical development. We took him to two years of Music Together classes, a fun, evidence-based way for family members and young children to interact in making music verbally, with instruments, and through movement. Whenever we sang, Kalani joined in the fun. With musical genes on both sides of the family, sometimes Kalani would sing chorus songs by heart, which made us all laugh, and Kalani's favorite was the tune, "Seize the Day." As Kalani became older, he became involved in musical theatre productions at his elementary/middle school. He took a few tap and jazz dance classes, but focused primarily on ballet with dance classes at Princeton Ballet School with several teachers including Mary Pat Robertson, and years of piano lessons with Taiwanese-American pianist Fang-Ting Liu.

Ironically, while on sabbatical in Taiwan, Kalani had his first night out courtesy of his uncle and aunt in Taipei. Baba and Dad spent the night watching and listening to the Taipei Gay Men's Chorus, G-Major. The G-Major guys were great singers, talented dancers, and had a wonderful sense of humor in multiple languages. The big difference between NJGMC and G-Major was that their concerts were invitation-only because many members were closeted. The need to protect members' identities was paramount.

In later years, Lance left the chorus to do his doctorate and a few years later I, too, went off in search of other pursuits. We both found massage and yoga with other gay men to be welcome additions to our lives. And after failed childhood swim lessons where I was afraid to put my face in the water, I became an avid swimmer. Date night for us became a time to try out new restaurants and bubble tea venues sometimes in NYC and Philly or a quick drive to the Shore and Asbury Park's burgeoning arts, indy film (The Showroom), coffee/teahouse/cat cafe (Catsbury Park), and local/sustainable/

organic food scene. Nurturing our relationship meant not only dad's night out but finding other gay friends near and far focused on music, politics, and bodywork as critical supports to strengthen our relationship and friendships as we continued the fight for more equitable laws for LGBTQ couples and families in the USA and Taiwan.

CHAPTER TWELVE

JUSTCVL

New Jersey Civil Union

In 2004, we became the second couple in Monroe Township to be granted new New Jersey domestic partnership benefits. There was a measly total of 9 benefits granted to lesbian and gay couples by New Jersey legislators and soon-to-be out (gay) and ex-(governor) Jim McGreevey. Yet estimates run to 1,100 as the total number of benefits that marriage gives to couples. So 9 benefits were a legal toe-hold that we hoped one day would expand to full marriage rights. We went to the Monroe Township clerk's office right away and became domestically partnered.

Only in New Jersey could a governor sign a domestic partnership bill; later come out of the closet as gay; resign office due to ethical trouble including alleged blackmail from an alleged lover he had put on the state payroll; find another gay man; fall in love; file for divorce; plan to enter the Episcopal priesthood; co-parent two children; and seek a civil union with his male partner courtesy of New Jersey legislators and governor Jon Corzine, who approved Civil Unions in late December 2007.

Stopping short of using the "M" word, the civil union legislation supposedly gave same-gender couples the same New Jersey state-level benefits of marriage, a huge increase from 2004's nine domestic partner benefits, but still shy of parity with heterosexual marriage, particularly at the federal level in terms of taxes, social security, and disability benefits. Nevertheless, we agreed that a civil union put our relationship and our family, including our ability to protect Kalani, on firmer legal ground. Civil Union benefits were greatly improved from the meager domestic partnership benefits we claimed in 2004 but still not equitable in terms of marriage rights. Again, we hoped that one day we would have access to full marriage equality as civil unions were a less than acceptable alternative.

Once we returned to New Jersey from sabbatical in Taiwan, we paid the $28 fee and had a public civil union ceremony performed by the mayor of Plainsboro, Peter Cantu, with my mom, Kalani, his cousin Ray from Taipei, and our friend and Plainsboro librarian Jenny Beckler as witnesses a few days after the anniversary of our original Chicago sacred commitment ceremony. We celebrated with a civil union cake at our annual summer party the following weekend, and we added a second vanity license plate to our other car: JUSTCVL joined DADSRUS. The significance of our entering into a Civil Union also showed our shifting attitudes about gay marriage. When we were childless, we didn't think much about the legal benefits of marriage as an institution but we were able and willing to critique its flaws as a sexist, classist, heterosexist institution over time.

But having gone through the adventurous process of becoming gay dads, we shifted our perspective about what gay marriage means for protecting children and both partners in a long-term relationship. It provides multiple benefits such as inheritance, the ability to have control over one's partner's health-care decision-making, social security/disability benefits should one partner die or develop a disability, and tax benefits that enhance the financial well-being of all family members. Another benefit for young children with same-gender parents is that marriage is easier to explain to young minds and hearts than the legal but confusing domestic partnership and civil union. As children of LGBTQ parents grow, they quickly learn the inequities and social injustices facing their parents and families denied the rights and privileges of marriage. But like other oppressed people, just because we are oppressed does not mean that we give up the struggle or have less pride in who we are and what we can do in our lives. Yet, we realized that single persons did not have access to many of these benefits and that marriage (or civil unions or domestic partnership) as an institution was not the ultimate answer to equitable treatment for all LGBTQ persons.

Gay marriage (in some countries) provided the chance for equitable benefits for couples and families with the same status as heterosexual couples. Yet, since the USA had a right-wing conservative power orientation for most of its history (with occasional outbursts of civil and human rights in the latter part of the 20th Century and in the beginning of the 21st Century), including Republicans and Democrats who happily supported Defense of Marriage bills in the late 90s, we questioned at that time how long it would take for marriage equality nationwide. We appreciated that only the Green Party had been pro-LGBT rights and marriage equality since its' founding in the USA in the mid-1980s. New Jersey's Governor Corzine was quoted in 2007 as saying gay marriage in New Jersey was "inevitable" but he didn't want to risk the Democrats' chances of losing the White House in 2008 over it. That gave us more reason to stay independent as voters who saw little true leadership and too many socially conservative forces in the major US political parties, backed by billionaires and their corporate media, with few exceptions.

We were not naive, however, to think that just because laws were passed that oppression targeting same-gender couples and same-gender parented families would cease. For example, up until that time, I had to pay annual imputed tax on Lance's health care benefits in New York State until we had a legal gay marriage--civil unions did not qualify as equal in the eyes of New York State tax law.

The other challenge was an international one--our ambivalence about the best time to pursue dual-national status for Kalani in Taiwan. Returning to the United States from Taiwan and being "civilly unioned," Lance had the paperwork ready and one day I drove Lance and Kalani to the Taipei Economic and Cultural Office (like a consulate or embassy but since Taiwan lacks formal recognition as a country, it goes by a different name) in New

York City to apply officially. But it wasn't that simple. They requested that their sister office in Atlanta had to verify the original birth certificate because Kalani was born in North Carolina, and it would need to be translated into Mandarin. Plus, my Mandarin name would have to be officially validated at the office in New York City.

It was obvious through emails and phone calls that our family was breaking new legal ground in Taiwan. We knew of gay parents who had applied for dual national citizenship for their children but they had either applied as single or with the name of a surrogate on the birth certificate, and that was not the case for us. Meanwhile, Lance and Kalani spent the rest of the day at Central Park Zoo, saw Tango, Roy and Silo (gay penguin dads and their daughter at the penguin house), and enjoyed the rest of the day. Later, we decided it would be easier to return to Taiwan and apply for Kalani's dual-national status in person with both of us present and all authenticated birth certificates in hand.

Like Roy & Silo, we had one child, so we were often asked by strangers, friends, and family: "Are you having any more kids? No was our consistent answer. The story of how Kalani came into our lives was unique and a one-time offer from Aunt Alison. We have assisted children and adolescents of other families professionally for decades in our careers, but our personal limit was one for many reasons. We decided saving for retirement was a more important goal than having a second child and that in our early 40s, we did not have the energy for parenting a second child while both working full-time jobs. We also felt the planet was better off with limiting our parenting to one.

That reasoning, however, didn't stop one of Kalani's New Jersey preschool teachers from lobbying us to have more children. She said that we were terrific parents and that she would love to have another one of our kids in class because Kalani and we were a lot of fun. But as sweet as that feedback was, we explained that Kalani's presence in the world was unique and that was fine with us. Plus, any more kids and we couldn't afford pre-school!

We focused on our hopes and dreams for Kalani's future and how best to navigate the world as a rainbow family. Some of the issues we continued to deal with in Taiwan were constant stares, comments, and two questions: Are you married (to either or us)? Where is Kalani's mother? As Kalani has matured, become taller, and traveled in major cities, those questions lessened except when we travel to rural areas of Taiwan where they persist.

In the USA, we received some stares, but the bigger challenge was how best to affirm mixed-race, multilingual, LGBTQ, and dual-national family identities. How little recognition there is, and even fewer media images, for mixed-race and multilingual persons and families (let alone LGBTQ mixed-race and multilingual families), although the numbers are rising according to census figures. We followed the 2008 presidential elections with interest but were dismayed at the poor quality of discussion and media mishandling of President Obama's mixed-race background.

On a happier note, when we returned from Taiwan sabbatical, a friend in Kalani's preschool told us about a new independent school that had just opened in the Princeton area. Ying-Hua International School was the first Mandarin-immersion, dual-language, Pre-K-8 school with International Baccalaureate curriculum in the area. While we had planned on Kalani attending public schools, and we had moved to Plainsboro for their public-school system featuring Mandarin, this posed a dilemma. Should we wait for Kalani to start part-time Mandarin classes in 4th grade in the public schools supplemented with Sunday Taiwanese school lessons, or add to his Mandarin language skills immediately by enrolling full-time in the new dual-language immersion school for cultural and linguistic immersion in Mandarin? We contacted the school, met the director, made a visit, and decided it would be the ideal place for Kalani.

We enrolled two months after we had the last confrontation with the prior local Montessori school's administrator's inept heterosexism. Their forms used mom and dad and when I repeatedly ask that they change them she refused. So, we refused to have our son in a school where administrators were rigid and unwilling to validate our identities as gay dads.

The first thing the administrator of Kalani's new pre-school and early elementary, Joy Zhao, wanted to know was what had happened at the other school that had bothered us. After sharing the story, the first thing she did was to ensure all of her written and online school materials used parent and/or guardian terminology in Mandarin and English, and Lance helped create accurate terminology in Mandarin for YingHua International English-Chinese School of Princeton (which started in Lawrenceville, moved to Princeton, and now is located in Kingston, NJ).

It felt wonderful to be welcomed to a school that celebrated all of our family's cultural and linguistic identities and had teachers and administrators who valued gay families, dual language education, and internationalism in action.

As a new small school, there were many opportunities to collaborate with teachers and administrators. For example, we wanted to ensure during the Unit of Inquiry on families that there were appropriate books about same-gender families and family diversity. We sent our list and the director had checked a bunch of them out of the library and ensured they were used in all classes. Another time, however, one of the teachers was doing a family tree unit and assigned grandparental names for students to use without realizing that there had been a mistake. In Taiwanese culture, maternal grandparents are usually referred to in Mandarin as "outer" grandparents because traditionally women are married into men's families. Lance discovered an error--his side of the family was referred to as "outer" by the teacher--he corrected it. Instead, he asked that all teachers refer to both sets of Kalani's grandparents in a generic way (as is done for paternal grandparents), since Kalani has two dads and two sets of paternal grandparents. The teachers were open to Lance's suggestion and it added to their credibility as they heard and acted on our feedback.

We helped Kalani be proud of all of his identities and to learn about what it means to be mixed-race and to honor all of his heritage, languages, ethnicities, and culture. That's not always an easy journey. In Taiwan, there's a internalized racism and privileging of persons with light skin and European features, at times, which can lead to exoticization. Light skin is often prized as a "look" but not necessarily by persons who are indigenous and/or celebrate their Taiwanese national and ethnic identities.

Yet, in the USA, racism takes a different form and Kalani heard "Why are you so dark?" from two different USA friends (one Asian and one White). Often in the USA we encountered adults who would say to us "I think Asian and European mixed people are the cutest of all." A response that each of us gave is: "I think all races are equally cute." The challenge was helping Kalani celebrate all of whom he is and not be side-tracked or exoticized in either Taiwan or the USA from less-than-affirming people and experiences. Instead, we focused on Kalani's strengths, family, and skills in negotiating and celebrating diverse ethnic, racial, linguistic, and family identities. As Kalani matured into adolescence, he had greater awareness of the stares and the racism targeting Asian bodies in the USA, the demasculinizing and desexualizing of Asian men and especially Asian gay men in the USA, and the intersectional challenges of racism, beautyism, linguicism, and immigrationism.

We have helped Kalani celebrate multiple identities through intentionally finding culturally diverse role models and experiences. Just before we left for sabbatical in Taiwan, we learned that friend Dr. Pauline Park would be having a documentary filmed about her life as a transgender activist. The filmmaker, Prof. Larry Tung, at the time faculty at Kean University, was documenting her closest friends, including those who knew her in Chicago. We were included and in the Summer of 2008, we attended the premiere of *Envisioning Justice: The Journey of a Transgender Woman* in Manhattan. While Kalani didn't necessarily understand the significance of being in a movie as part of a mixed-race gay-headed household, we were happy to add our voices to Pauline's story and celebrate her accomplishments. Kalani stole the show during the filming by dancing the entire time on our laps.

Pride month 2008 would not have been complete without marching in the NYC pride parade, which we missed the prior year due to time in Taiwan. We marched with GAPIMNY, - and the guys created and carried a traditional Chinese dragon. Once we began to march, we wove - our way under the dragon for most of the parade route. This was a great way to distract Kalani, who kept trying to leave the parade because he wanted to watch it more than march. But he handled the six-mile trip well. We took some time out to watch the parade from the side once it started raining and ended by marching with the Taiwanese women's group at the end of the parade. Of course, that left time to explain the go-go boys float and how some LGBTQ adults were allowed to dance in their underwear on floats during Gay Pride but not children.

After the parade, we were interviewed by the *World Journal,* the largest Mandarin-language daily paper in the USA. We were less than thrilled, however, to discover that a Chinese website used the article to sell sex toys and lube with only hot white models. We didn't have a problem with what they were selling but the ad should have had racially diverse men, particularly Asians; sexy comes in all shapes, sizes, and colors.

Soon after that interview, *Gay Parent Magazine* requested a follow-up article about us for their tenth anniversary year. I responded with written words and Lance responded with pictures for the interview. We were featured on the cover for a third time with a fun retrospective of pictures from past issues regarding Kalani's birth and our Chicago sacred commitment ceremony and a picture of our JUSTCVL and DADSRUS license plates.

Another question that we often received as Kalani was growing up was how we talk about Kalani's origins with Kalani. We have always been open from the start about how Kalani came into the world. The first pictures in Kalani's baby photo album are of Aunt Alison pregnant with Kalani inside her uterus. As gay men, we both knew the pain of growing up without adequate information about our sexuality and did not want to repeat that experience for Kalani who had the security and clarity of knowing how they came into the world from the first day Kalani saw the pictures in the first photo album. We wanted to ensure Kalani had the age-apporpriate information about sexuality and his unique origins throughout childhood and adolescence. Our commitment to sharing our story is to help other same-gender couples and families, particularly in countries that lack LGBTQ rights, can find the resources they need to celebrate and empower their multiple identities and parenting.

Sometimes, sharing our story starts at home with perfect strangers. After our experience with the stolen rainbow flag and our allies who helped fly multiple flags in New Rochelle, we had kept our rainbow flag under wraps for our first five years in New Jersey. But I decided that it was time to fly something other than the Earth flag at our home and so the Rainbow flag came out of the closet for pride month in June of 2008 in Plainsboro. My mom made a funny comment about it, since this was the first time that she was living with us that we had it flying outside. She asked, "Are you sure you want everyone to know about your sexual orientation by flying that outside?" I laughed and said, "Well, the flag is really about celebrating LGBTQ pride, but if everyone doesn't already know, that's fine by me." A couple of days later, mom was still not quite convinced, "I'm not sure it's a good thing to have that flag flying out there because it might stir up trouble." I said, "Mom, do you remember what happened in New Rochelle with our neighbors when our flag was stolen and they suggested that everyone fly the flags as a gesture of solidarity? Why live a life of fear, when we can live a life based on love and pride in who we are and the accomplishments of LGBTQ people?"

One night toward the end of the month, there was a knock on the door and Lance answered it. A young gay man was strolling through the town center neighborhood where we lived and saw the rainbow flag and the DADSRUS license plate and decided he had to introduce himself as he didn't know any other gay men in our town, let alone ones that might be a couple or have a child. He and his boyfriend had been together for a year but they'd just had a disagreement and he was inspired by what he saw and enough of an extrovert to knock on the door. In our early 20s, this was something that neither of us would have seen nor done.

The telling and re-telling of our story can provide inspiration and courage for Kalani at times when life may not treat him fairly or kindly. It's an honor to be a queer family and to be Kalani's allies on the journey toward adulthood. Yet even as LGBTQ advocates, too often in Kalani's school settings we found we had to struggle with intensive advocacy on LGBTQ and dual language issues.

CHAPTER THIRTEEN

MANDARIN IMMERSION PART 2

DUAL-LANGUAGE CHALLENGES

In late 2009, Kalani was enrolled in YingHua International School for a third year and had become so fluent in Mandarin verbally that teachers considered him a native speaker. Kalani's reading and writing skills, while not on par with other Mandarin-speaking first graders around the world, were advancing. I had served a second year as president of the YingHua Family Association and enjoyed supporting the school's hardworking and underpaid teachers and other parents and guardians.

Yet, even though it was a gay-friendly school, we were the only same-gender parents, and Kalani was, true to the research on gay-headed families, comfortable with gender-nontraditional interests. Kalani, being a movement maven, had become quite the dancer. He started a third year of mixed ballet classes and a first year of tap dance class along with a world music class outside of school. His interest in dance brought some teasing for the first time in his first-grade year from some traditional male classmates.

We heard about it and told the teacher and head of school and the school responded in support of Kalani by taking the entire school to see a local dance studio ballet performance, which was a terrific gesture to help see the athleticism of dance. But as the year ended, Kalani didn't want to dance any more, which he had enjoyed since he fell in love with Fancy Dancing at a Native American Indian Pow-Wow at age two. Something was off. We spent the summer giving Kalani permission to fall back in love with dance. Kalani took a two-week piano camp in addition to the annual summer Mandarin immersion camp and reconnected with dance.

But what amazed us was Kalani's jump in English skills. Even with only about 10% of the day at YingHua in English instruction, Kalani, who couldn't get enough of picture books in the fall, had proceeded with such speed into chapter books that Kalani was reading several a day by the summer of 2010 and became interested in upper elementary and middle school books by the end of first grade. This convinced us the dual-language approach, small class sizes, and large numbers of teachers had catapulted Kalani's learning in unexpected ways.

Also in the Fall of 2009, a group of YingHua International parents and staff began discussing bringing this dual language Mandarin immersion model with International Baccalaureate into a larger public school setting. A group of 12 founders formed and began the process to create New Jersey's first Mandarin Immersion/IB charter school. While I was not a fan of charter schools and I am opposed to for-profit charters, I agreed to help when the group decided to pursue the charter path. Princeton International Academy Charter School (PIACS) charter was written after 5 weeks of sleepless nights by YHIS Director Joy Zhao, YHIS Founder Dr. Bonnie Liao, and me. New Jersey had announced in late August of 2009 that it would open a fast-track process for people to apply to create and open a school in less than a year's time and 12 of us took that challenge.

By the summer of 2010, full enrollment and waiting lists for future spots in the incoming K-2 cohort of 170 students had been identified, staff had been interviewed, a location had been found, and the school was on the verge of opening in the Fall of 2010. The state had approved the plan in January of 2010 citing the need for the curriculum in the three districts it covered (Princeton, West-Windsor/Plainsboro, and South Brunswick) and the financial plan soundness. What founders hadn't expected was the pushback from the three districts' superintendents and boards of education. What ensued was a public relations battle between forces interested in change and forces in public school districts that had a good reputation but achievement gaps that were not dealt with in all three districts affecting Latinx and African American students.

In the fall of 2009 the three districts were given the plans for PIACS and all raised concerns against the idea. As the year wore on, the invective and misinformation emanating from two of the districts—Princeton and West-Windsor/Plainsboro was excessive. The Princeton superintendent, a White woman, in a district infamous for achievement gaps, accused PIACS of "segregation," even though 75% of the founders were people of color—an even mix of Asian-Americans and African-Americans, and high numbers of enrollees were from bilingual families, families of color, and first-generation immigrant families of varied ethnic and racial identities. In West Windsor-Plainsboro, the district where we lived, anonymous racist threats were made toward Chinese/Taiwanese parents, Chinese/Taiwanese founders, and the Chinese/Taiwanese children of founders. I could handle pushback against me, but going after Kalani (and other kids) was beyond out of bounds. Both districts' boosters engaged in a scorched-earth policy of scaring parents into thinking the remaining public schools would be "irreparably harmed," to use one board member's words, if PIACS opened.

But it wasn't until mid-summer 2010 that the districts played their hand. PIACS had identified a one-year lease in an old seminary that was being converted to K-12 school usage and wanted to begin a year early. The districts hired high-powered attorneys who found a tiny error in the application and pounced at the zoning board meeting threatening at the 11th hour to sue the zoning board if they went through with the hearing for a zoning variance. The Zoning Board caved and PIACS was left to wait a year before it could open. This meant 170 families, including ours, had to scramble at the last minute to find a school for their children to attend.

I was appalled and saddened at the threats targeting Kalani (and the other Chinese/Taiwanese children of founders) from anonymous district boosters; it had become unsafe to move Kalani to public school in that environment and even though our family strongly supports public schools. district boosters. turned neighbors against neighbors and PIACS families reported they were shunned by others simply for seeking to attend PIACS.

I had helped write the mission statement for PIACS to include concepts of equity, peace, and social justice, and only one other school in the area came close to what we sought. We contacted Princeton Friends School (PFS) as they had a commitment to inquiry-based teaching, peace, equality, nonviolence, environmental and arts education, and some world languages. With Kalani all about science and the arts, this appeared the best choice. Upon contacting the school, we learned that they had a few two-mom families and Kalani would no longer be alone in the LGBT-headed family department—a first in five schools attended.

But we worried when told there were no spots for second graders and that they would assess Kalani for third-grade placement. Kalani was assessed at a third-grade level in all subjects and transferred from Yinghua (having aged out as at the time the school had not expanded in grade levels) to the closest school offering inquiry-based dual-language education that didn't require us to move. Kalani also started Spanish at the end of the Spring semester at YingHua and continued at PFS. While PFS offered Mandarin, it was at a beginning level and Kalani shifted to after-school Mandarin at YingHua instead. Lance spoke Mandarin at home with Kalani to attempt to bridge the gap, and Kalani enrolled in a summer Mandarin immersion program near home and in Taiwan when we traveled over the summer. PIACS suffered a similar fate with a different township's zoning board a year later losing by one vote and did not open.

After a year of doing Mandarin at PFS, the teacher's style was old-fashioned and not a good fit, so Kalani switched to a strong Spanish teacher at PFS and we hired a tutor to revive his Mandarin skills. After another year, Kalani restarted weekend Princeton Chinese Language School (PCLS) lessons, where he originally began prior to our sabbatical in Taiwan. Run by Taiwanese, this school taught traditional characters, arts and culture programs, and rotated different Taiwanese food vendors/restaurateurs who sold traditional food every Sunday encouraging the local Taiwanese community to descend on the school to buy traditional take-out dishes to keep families happy at school and during the week. But the challenge with PCLS was that not all the students were interested in speaking Mandarin, classroom management skills varied, and instruction depended on the skills of the volunteer adults who taught classes, most of whom had no background in language education. Kalani struggled memorizing and retaining Mandarin characters outside an immersion school program. Lacking the daily reinforcement of speaking and reading Mandarin, Kalani's

Spanish skills soared but his Mandarin plateaued at an elementary level. After six years in the weekend Chinese school, we withdrew Kalani at the end of 8th grade to focus on other activities. Kalani had elementary conversational fluency in Mandarin and continued Spanish in high school at an advanced level. As powerful advocates for Kalani's learning opportunities, we reflected on how different it was for us growing up with our fathers in Taichung and Park Forest, IL..

CHAPTER FOURTEEN

SAYING GOODBYE TO OUR DADS

Neither Lance nor I were close to our fathers growing up. My dad, Charles Marshall Hayes, was born in Blanford, IN and raised in rural Indiana near Terre Haute. He was an only child who was intellectual and had been teased by other kids for being so bright (advanced 2 grades in elementary school) and artistic. He was a professional pilot having earned his pilot's license before a driver's license at age 16, and a member of the OX-5 club, the Experimental Aircraft Association.

After he met my mom, Lois Irene Farquharson, (and had sold the '57 Thunderbird and replaced it with a station wagon to lure a wife—my dad was definitely straight!), he knew the poor pay for pilots was not enough to raise a family. He returned to school to complete graduate credits at the University of Chicago to compliment his bachelor's degree in sociology from Indiana State and became a high school librarian and later a current events/sociology teacher at Rich East High School in Park Forest, IL.

He taught private pilot lessons on the side at Frankfort (IL) Airport and flew until his health declined in his early 70s. His father, Curtis, was a traveling salesperson who was emotionally and physically abusive. His mother, Hazel, handled a variety of jobs and eventually commuted in her early 50s for a master's degree in library science from the University of Illinois. She and Curtis moved to Michigan where she was named Michigan librarian of the year in the mid-1960s for her work in securing a $1 million dollar donation from businessperson Ray Herrick to create a new library in Holland, MI. She then worked as a medical librarian until her retirement at age 80 at Ingalls Memorial Hospital in Harvey, IL and lived near us in Park Forest, IL.

When my dad retired from high school teaching, there were early signs of dementia. Years later when my parents agreed to move in with us in New Jersey, it had advanced to Alzheimer's disease. Six months before my dad died, my mom had done all she could for care at home and dad went into a memory care/assisted living unit. The night he died I was teaching practicum class with future school counseling students and mom called to tell me the news. I didn't cry and my students were shocked and could not understand why. I explained that I had grieved his loss decades before, that we were not close, and that people grieve in different ways (and being English and Scot ethnicities I was not one for public displays of emotion even with my students). In reflecting on the positive aspect of my dad's presence in my life, he modeled a love of politics, current affairs/sociology, nature, singing, classical music, and dogs.

We did a brief memorial service for my dad in our home in Plainsboro, and Alison, Lance, Kalani and I sprinkled dad's ashes both by a tree near Carnegie Lake in Princeton as he loved the water and sailing, and by a tree in our backyard on Sullivan Street as he had no desire for the expense of a traditional funeral or belief in a religious ceremony.

Lance's dad, Mu-chung Chen, was born one of three siblings to a poor family in Fujian province of southeastern China. He married Lance's mom, Bi–Lan Hsiao, in China, and had two children by the time they fled the Communist uprising with her parents for Taiwan after losing everything to robbers along the way. Bi-Lan's father was a doctor, herbalist, and calligrapher, and his wife a homemaker. Unable to find jobs in Taiwan, Lance's dad enrolled in a police academy to become a police officer and worked for decades in Taichung before his retirement. Lance's mom was a homemaker who sold cigarettes on the side to support the family. Having grown up in a wealthy family in China as an only child--unusual at the time--Lance's mom had to adjust to a difficult life in Taiwan.

Lance's dad was married into his wife's family. with an understanding that the first five children, if they had them, had to have the surname Hsiao, Lance's mom's family name. The last four children then had his dad's surname, Chen. If Lance had been born among the first five siblings rather than #9, we would have been the Hsiao-Hayes family. Lance's dad was a traditional patriarch and used both emotional and physical abuse toward Lance; not a safe environment. At home, however, things were less than orderly. With nine children total, and one to two in-laws in a tiny two-room police housing unit, living was difficult. Most of Lance's siblings were raised by his maternal grandmother in the apartment.

Lance's remembers his dad being physically and emotionally abusive to him and his siblings, but not all of his siblings experienced their father that way nor do they have similar memories. Lance was not close to his father and was not afraid to speak his mind but hated the consequences. He often stayed with his older siblings and eventually won a scholarship to an independent school in Taichung, which allowed him to focus more on his studies and away from the chaos at home. Similarly, being the top student in his Ming Dao high school class allowed Lance to enter and graduate from National Taiwan University in Taipei, which meant he could live far from the drama of his dad while attending college. When Lance had the chance, he immigrated to the USA on a work-study program to attend New York University for graduate school in physical therapy.

Years later, when Lance's dad developed dementia, Lance and I supported his parents with an annual payment to assist with health care and living expenses, as many of Lance's siblings had done prior to their retirement. When Lance's dad died, Lance returned to Taichung, Taiwan alone for the funeral and to support his mom and siblings while I stayed back with Kalani and my mom. Lance, when he returned, said he was able to thank his father's spirit and forgive him at the funeral. For the first time, Lance appreciated the gifts of life and financial support while reconciling and forgiving the abuse.

Lance's dad had a traditional Christian ceremony and burial in Taichung, Taiwan and was buried in the Hsiao-Chen family garden on a Western mountain overlooking what were once farmer's fields and now stands the Taichung technical park sprouting electronics and technology plants.

Back in New Jersey, Kalani wasn't sure he could make it through two weeks of my cooking, but Lance made dishes before he left and we survived on my limited kitchen skills in Lance's absence. In both cases when our dads died, we helped Kalani grieve by writing a letter about each of our fathers, reading it aloud, and helping Kalani create a scrapbook of pictures and mementos to help remember his grandfathers.

Our dads met only once in Chicago when Lance's parents visited the USA for the first of two trips. Lance and I stayed clear of our dads for most of our lives. We were close to our moms as they were comfortable with non-traditional sons although our dads accepted us when we came out. With the deaths of our fathers, it gave us time to reflect on the contrasting encouragement, love, and advocacy roles that our mothers consistently hold in our lives.

CHAPTER FIFTEEN

HONORING OUR MOMS

My mom, Lois Irene Farquharson Hayes, was born in Buffalo, NY to a first generation Scot, William Farquharson, who was a supervisor at a steel mill, and Edith Jane Logan, also of Scottish descent and a kindergarten teacher. Mom was a non-traditional girl from the start with no interest in girls' activities. She horrified her Kindergarten teacher when at playtime all the other girls went after the dolls. But not mom. She only wanted to make things with the construction tools and couldn't wait to build in class.

Mom went to Mt. Holyoke for her undergraduate degree in Botany and then graduated with a PhD in plant science at Indiana University where she studied with botanist Dr. Paul Weatherwax. At one point she took a trip around the world, in part so she could spend some time as his research assistant for a couple of weeks in Thailand. After she graduated she took a job teaching at Franklin College in Indiana and it was when she was there that she met my father Charlie, who had grown up and lived west of Indianapolis. My mom appreciated my dad because he was the only man she ever dated who liked her for her intelligence. As a woman doing a doctorate in the sciences in the 1950s, she knew her chances for marriage were slim, especially once she was out on her own teaching as an assistant professor of botany in rural Indiana south of Indianapolis.

After giving birth two children and raising us for a decade, mom decided that she was ready to re-engage her brain but knew that the field of botany had changed drastically in her decade away and that she couldn't return to it. Instead, following the lead of her husband and her mother-in-law, she returned to graduate school for a master's in library science at Rosary College (now Dominican University) in River Forest, IL. She became medical librarian, until she retired, a few minutes from home at the Chicago College of Osteopathy's southern branch in Olympia Fields, IL.

Mom was a key figure in supporting our family for over two decades both physically and financially once she and dad moved from Illinois to the East Coast. We co-owned homes in Monroe Township and Plainsboro, N and our current townhome in Newtown, PA. Her physical support on the ground whenever we've needed it and sharing finances on housing allowed us to provide resources for Kalani that would not have been possible otherwise, and for that we are forever grateful. Plus, her dry sense of humor was always lurking, often when we least expected it.

Yet, physical challenges have begun to take a toll in the last few years. She fell 4 times and broke an ankle, a wrist, had a compression fracture of her spine. In October of 2018, after fainting at home, she had double emergency pacemaker surgery within 12 hours of her heart stopping twice in one night at the local hospital in Langhorne, PA. She healed remarkably after each fall, but we are thankful to be in a townhome with an elevator, which has been a necessity with her health challenges. To honor her for all that she has done for our family we organized a surprise 90th birthday luncheon bash for her in October of 2017 at Rats Restaurant on the Grounds for Sculpture campus in Hamilton, NJ, with her daughter Alison and other assorted relatives, friends, and family appreciating her presence in our lives. Mom's favorite activities include: nutrition, buying and selling stocks, and daily meditation for over 45 years as a member of Self-Realization Fellowship.

Lance's mom, Bi-Lan Hsiao, grew up in the wealthiest family in her small town in southeastern China's Fujian province the only child of a highly creative man skilled in calligraphy and many other talents who was the town's medical doctor. When Lance's mom reached school age, she had to walk a long distance to another town for school. Not wanting her to suffer the long walk every day, her father set up a school in their hometown for her and other children. When her father met Lance's dad, her father appreciated his hard work ethic and talents so he decided to let his only child marry him.

However, the marriage was on the condition that he marry into HER family (very unusual in patriarchal Chinese culture) and that their first few children all take Lance's mom's family name, Hsiao, and any additional children (there were four and Lance was the youngest) would take his dad's surname, Chen. The story of how they made it from China to Taiwan during the fall of the Nationalists in China and the retreat to Taiwan was harrowing. Her parents lost everything and as a wealthy family that was especially painful. They were robbed and attacked and after more than one incident realized that their lives were in danger in China and that their only escape, now with two children and her parents, was to flee to Taiwan.

Lance's mom had nine children over two decades. She always was most fond of Lance as he was her baby. When I came to visit the first time, we had an instant connection even though we had few words for each other but the nonverbals said it all. She always considered me her 8th son and 10th child and my mom, Lois, always viewed Lance as her second son and third child. 8,000 miles, two languages, and two different cultures, our moms, the same age, had remarkable similarities although their own life trajectories were polar opposites.

One big difference for us has been living with my mom for the past 16 years, and only visiting Lance's mom every two years or so in Taichung. The challenges have been at a distance as Lance's mom's health has faded. She has lived with Alzheimer's disease for over 10 years and recently had heart failure. Lance, as the only doctoral-level health-care professional in his family, has been a family health consultant via Facetime and over the phone countless times with siblings and his mom's health aide, A-he.

Lance has helped make healthcare decisions in her best interests and challenged inappropriate medical care on numerous occasions. For example, recently he asked A-he to list all the prescriptions his mom had been prescribed by the pulmonologist and the cardiologist. When he ran all 10 prescriptions through a pharmaceutical search engine to check drug interactions, he found two had severe interactions. He asked A-he to stop his mom taking them, and asked her to take all 10 bottles to both physicians.

Neither doctor had asked nor checked to see what the other doctor had prescribed and the hospital pharmacist had not noticed the dangerous interactions. After a series of falls in her townhome built with the money Lance's dad made as a police offer and designed and built by her son the architect, her Alzheimer's disease entered a final stage. Ironically, she can recognize others at times accurately but phases in and out of lucidity. She remains emotionally present, however, so when Lance and his siblings met in October of 2018 and agreed that it was time for her to move to a small apartment with an elevator and sell the townhome, with the proceeds paying for her remaining healthcare, she was angry.

But at age 91, the risks of her falling down the stairs were too great to not make a safer housing transition to an apartment building in northern Taichung city. She made the move successfully and enjoys the views on a high floor overlooking northern Taichung. The stories of our moms and their creativity and tenacity in the midst of life challenges on both sides of the family foreshadow the next generation.

CHAPTER SIXTEEN

EMPOWERING THE NEXT GENERATION

When Kalani was young, Lance was pretty sure that he would turn out to be gay. I didn't want to make any assumptions and we were fine with wherever Kalani would land on the sexuality spectrum as long as he was honest and happy. But as Kalani grew, I also became convinced that the next generation would be a child of the rainbow. Maybe it started with the first time Kalani announced he was going to get married. It was during his time at the local Montessori pre-school when he said on the car ride home, "I want to get married to Gianna (a girl in his class)," and when asked "Anyone else?" he said, "Om! (a boy in his class)." While that sentence alone was not a confirmation, it raised our curiousity as gay dads. Later, at age 5 Kalani was in the same ballet class as Gianna and when Lance mentioned that Kalani had said years earlier that he wanted to marry Gianna, Kalani responded, "But I want to marry a boy now!"

Having spent years teaching human sexuality and working as a sexuality counselor, and as gay men, we have been honest with Kalani about his origins and shared our lives as out gay dads from the start. Kalani attended gay pride parades, gay chorus concerts, and had the chance to meet kids and parents in other LGBTQ-headed households. Kalani had many books to read with LGBTQ families, and three Robie Harris & Michael Emberley human sexuality children's picture books (*It's Not The Stork, It's So Amazing!,* and *It's Perfectly Normal*) that explained, using cartoon formats, developmentally appropriate sexuality education messages.

Sometimes when sharing our perception that Kalani seemed to be leaning toward same-gender interests, we'd get surprised looks from gay and lesbian friends. Similarly, some heterosexuals around us were surprised. Others were most affirming—just like our own experiences of coming out. Regardless of sexual orientation, some adults have a hard time seeing children as sexual beings or having the capacity to know their attractions. Yet, heterosexual children are rarely questioned about this and too many adults still assume that's how most kids are/will be. At age 6, Kalani announced the following to one or both of us at different times (especially on the drive to or from school—something about car rides to and from school that always brought interesting moments):

- "I want to be a gay boy so I can marry another boy but if I don't find one I like, I'll marry Hong Hong (a girl in Kalani's class), because she's so sweet and nice to me."
- "I have two choices in life—to be gay or lesbian."
- "I work differently than other human beings."
- "I want to marry Tyler (boy at a birthday party) because he's nice to me."
- "I wish to be gay because gay is the best."

- "I wish Thea (a girl in Kalani's class) was a boy instead of a girl so we could be gay or lesbians."
- "I want to be the first person in our family to be a lesbian."
- "I wish our family was all gay or lesbian because there are too many families that are 'he' gender and 'she' gender." I then said, "But some of our family IS gay." Kalani replied, "Yes, baba, daddy, and me."

One of the confirmatory moments that Kalani had same-gender interests was the first day Kalani used the word gay to refer to himself. We were riding in the car to YingHua International School and Kalani exclaimed (at age 6):

- "Daddy, I choose to be gay so I can marry a boy in my class but I don't like any of the boys in my class because none of them have teeth that look as good as mine."

It was all I could do to keep the car under control and not burst out laughing, but somehow Kalani was given reassurances that he could marry whomever he wanted and that six year olds were too young to marry and that there was plenty of time to decide on who at a later date as an adult. I thanked Kalani for being so honest and real.

One day, Kalani, age 7, announced:

- "All the girls want to marry me. It's so annoying! I don't want to marry any of them. I want to marry a boy. I'm gay. I want to find a boy with a big tree so that we can build a treehouse together. I got it (being gay) from Baba and Daddy. I'm going to promise that I'm going to be gay forever even if I change my mind I'm going to be gay forever."

Kalani picked the right parents. Of course, Kalani's grandmother Lois was rather surprised when one day Kalani walked into her room at age 7 and announced to her he was gay. We had not said a word. She emerged and told me what Kalani had said and wondered if we had heard that (I assured her that Kalani had been sharing similar phrases about his sexual orientation with us for a couple of years prior). She asked the very same next question that she'd asked me when I'd come out to her as bisexual at age 21: "Are you sure he's old enough to know for sure?" I assured her that all we needed to do was to support Kalani at this time and in the future wherever Kalani was on the sexual identity journey.

A few days later mom found me on the front porch and had been thinking about this at length and asked, "Shouldn't we be helping Kalani to know who to tell and when so that he doesn't get hurt?" I said, "Well, Kalani is smart and going to a school where some teachers are LGBT and/or allies, so I expect no problems. But if there are, we will deal with them and help. But Kalani needs to be honest about who he is. If Kalani were to announce he was heterosexual, would you have the same concerns or treat Kalani similarly?"

While finding picture books for Kalani with gay and lesbian themes, characters, and families was easy, finding elementary-age chapter books was more difficult. There is a dearth of writing for kids who come out in elementary school and need to see their world, their love, and their hopes and dreams represented in developmentally appropriate ways. There is much to be written as more kids come out in elementary school following earlier cohorts of teens coming out in high school and middle school and youth in older elementary grades. After all, haven't heterosexuals always known from the earliest ages in early elementary school whom they wanted to marry?

It was with this idea that a group of my School Counselor Educator colleagues and I, in 2009, conceived the idea of Supporting Students Saving Lives as an annual LGBTQ youth conference for K-12 school counselors and educators, sponsored by the Center for Excellence in School Counseling and Leadership, that ran for four years, 2010-2013. For the second year of the conference, we discussed the need to provide panels of family members, particularly those with elementary- and middle-school students to share their journeys with children either living with LGBTQ parents and/or who had come out as LGBTQ. While GLSEN and others have worked relentlessly to start Gender Sexuality Alliances (GSAs) in many high schools in the USA and some other countries worldwide, we've lagged behind in most middle and elementary schools. Yet with Dr. Ritch Savin-Williams's research and many anecdotal reports, students are coming out earlier not only in high school but in elementary and middle school and need that social-emotional support.

However, living in the same school district (West Windsor-Plainsboro, NJ) as the two students who had bullied gay Rutgers University student Tyler Clementi prior to his committing suicide by jumping off the George Washington Bridge, we had a harsh local reminder of the life-threatening dangers harassment and bullying have on LGBTQ youth. It was at dinner one night when we were discussing the conference that Kalani asked, "Can I be on the family panel?" Lance and I looked at each other and without missing a beat, said "Sure, if you want to." Kalani did, and at that point, we as a family were confirmed presenters for the second Supporting Students/Saving Lives conference in San Diego, CA. Kalani presented on multiple LGBT-themed chapter and picture books at age 7.5 to a room full of adults who were in awe at Kalani's skill and comfort with so many books. That year in the conference session, Kalani also came out as gay during the presentation. We were amazed and proud. But after that public sharing, Kalani decided to not share with adults he didn't know about being gay. The following two years, our family was flown to the conference so that Kalani could reprise his part of the workshop with Dad and Baba as the sole elementary school-age presenter in the four-year duration of the conference.

Each year, we watched Kalani mature as a presenter in answering spontaneous questions from adults. Kalani began to realize how unique it was for an elementary school student to educate adult school counselors about what it was like living in an LGBT-headed family. There were many fun anecdotes and quotes from over the years raising a queer child while pursuing LGBTQ and marriage equality activism. Some of those moments with Kalani included:

— "I want girl drag from Santa this Xmas," said Kalani in 6th grade.
— "Grandma, do you have high heels I can wear?" Grandma Lois: "Sorry Kalani, I've never worn high heels…." when Kalani asked in 7th grade.
— Watching the TV series GLEE as a family for five years was inspirational.. Watching gay, lesbian, bisexual, and transgender youth characters of various ethnic/racial identities (Kurt, Blaine, Santana, Brittany, Unique) was a first in USA television and our family grew with the characters. Since we sing, it was an ideal series of teachable moments to discuss issues around school, sexuality, bullying, violence, and family diversity. And I had a slight family connection to GLEE having done my undergraduate degree at Indiana University when Ryan Murphy succeeded me on the features beat of the *Indiana Daily Student* newspaper.
— The never-ending battle to start a Gender-Sexuality Alliance (GSA) at Kalani's Quaker elementary/middle school. While we didn't succeed, we raised awareness and made some inroads in challenging the school to be more LGBTQ-inclusive, including having a rainbow flag hang among other flags in the multi-purpose hall, including more LGBTQ-themed books in the literature reading lists, adding more LGBTQ-themed books in the library, etc. We were excited for Kalani's entrance to a Quaker high school with a GSA, many out LGBTQ students and faculty including the head of school, to decrease isolation and increase support and affirmation..
— One of our favorite actions was in 2009 when we were one of the first LGBTQ and Asian families to march in the Lunar New Year parade in Manhattan. Prior to 2009 LGBTQ groups were banned from the parade

so this was a huge victory for LGBTQ Asian visibility in New York City. The downside was how cold the weather was in February compared to Taiwan. Since 2009 we have marched most years as a family either in the Manhattan or Flushing, Queens Lunar New Year parades with the LGBTQ Asian family group.

— We joined an Upper West Side NYC protest against the Hong Kong government when they appointed a reparative-therapy-affirming psychiatrist to do training for social workers and counselors in Hong Kong:

— https://pinkalliance.hk/gapimny-action-in-support-of-hk-lgbt-community/.

— I spoke at the Ridgewood, NJ memorial for Tyler Clementi, the closeted young gay Rutgers freshman who was bullied and committed suicide by jumping from the George Washington Bridge after believing his roommate had spied on him having sex with another man in his shared residence hall room. It disturbed and angered us that Tyler Clementi's perpetrator lived within walking distance of our Plainsboro, NJ home. I contacted various campus LGBTQ groups to see if they might co-sponsor something in Plainsboro but no one returned my calls. I spoke at the memorial as a member of the LGBTQ community, as a gay dad, and as a Plainsboro resident. I talked about my vision that one day it would be great to see a giant rainbow flag hung annually over the George Washington bridge in June during Gay Pride Month to honor the memory of Tyler and all LGBTQ youth. In 2016, Dharun Ravi, the perpetrator, and his attorney, filed a motion to have him exonerated on the charges because of a new ruling by the New Jersey Supreme court that, in part, challenged his conviction. In the end he pled guilty to one charge of attempted invasion of privacy a third-degree felony, but was never charged in connection with Tyler's suicide.

Kalani's emergence as queer and "2nd gen" has been a powerful and fun experience for us as gay dads. Kalani inspired us to push our advocacy further both in Taiwan and in the USA. Kalani was central to planning and participating in our NYC gay wedding and our 15-year renewal-of-vows.

CHAPTER SEVENTEEN

HUZBNDZ

NYC WEDDING & 15-YEAR RENEWAL OF VOWS

It was a sunny late summer afternoon in Manhattan with temperatures in the high 70s and hardly a cloud in the sky. At the edge of the Friends Meetinghouse on Rutherford Street in the East Village, singles and couples and families with children and grandchildren entered the historic red brick Friends Meetinghouse with sounds of laughter and chatter. Upon entering , guests were greeted by my mom and Kalani, who handed each guest a rainbow flag, a purple or pink feather boa, and an order of ceremony. When the meetinghouse doors closed, three voices--a high tenor, a booming baritone, and a deep alto, emerged from the choir loft on the second floor singing socialist Yip Harburg's "Somewhere Over the Rainbow" as Lance on guitar, Kalani, and I walked downstairs in matching black tuxedos with lavender vests. With our guests joining on the second verse, it was wall-to-wall grins as we sang our way to the front of the meetinghouse for our legal New York City gay wedding and 15-year renewal of vows conducted by the Rev. Raymond Rodriguez, a new gay dad in a mixed-race relationship and an interfaith minister:

"Somewhere over the rainbow way up high

There's a land that I heard of once in a lullaby

Somewhere over the rainbow skies are blue

And the dreams that you dare to dream really do come true

Someday I'll wish upon a star

And wake up where the clouds are far

Behind me

Where troubles melt like lemon drops

Away above the chimney tops

That's where you'll find me

Somewhere over the rainbow bluebirds fly

Birds fly over the rainbow.

Why then, oh, why can't I?

If happy little bluebirds fly

Beyond the rainbow.

Why, oh, why can't I?"

The Rev. Rodriguez spoke about the importance of the ceremony for us as a couple and family:

"Good afternoon. It gives me great pleasure to be here today...a very special day where we celebrate with Stuart and Lance the renewal of their vows and their family with their son Kalani. On behalf of this couple I would like to also give a warm welcome to all the loved ones who are gathered here today. This day is made perfect because you are present here today. You have been invited to be part of this celebration because you are cherished and loved by Lance, Stuart and Kalani and hold a very special place in their hearts. The gifts of love, support, and friendship that you have shared with this couple are what has supported them to grow and be the persons they are today. On their behalf I welcome you and I thank you for being here today."

"Today's celebration of love has been a journey of 17 years. Lance and Stuart met in January of 1995 and from their first date it was evident that they shared much in common, most notably their values, appreciation of differences, and deep commitment to equity and social justice in their relationship, family, and within the larger community. When they were children, neither Stuart nor Lance dreamed of having a long-term relationship or even having a child of their own. But as life would have it, they share their love and commitment of 17 years, are devoted parents to Kalani, are dutifully engaged in challenging the norm through political activism and, as they are doing today, publicly share their love for each other and family."

"On June 28th, 1997 in Chicago, Stuart and Lance had a sacred commitment ceremony at a time when nowhere in the world was gay marriage legally recognized. It was important for this couple to have a public ceremony to honor their relationship and bring their families together regardless of legal recognition. The theme of their ceremony then was a poem by Chinese poet Lu Yu, whose message was "Who can stop us from celebrating?" And that is exactly what they have been doing ever since."

"When in June of this year New York state finally recognized gay marriage, Lance and Stuart decided to continue to support their family with a renewal of vows and strengthen their legal standing and as couple and family with a state-recognized marriage. Lance and Stuart chose this beautiful location, the Friends Meetinghouse, in honor of their appreciation for the Quaker values of simplicity, peace, integrity, community, equity, and stewardship."

"So what does love have to do with it? Everything! Love has sustained their relationship over the past 17 years. For Stuart and Lance continue to give their hearts to each other in the knowledge that each will always carry the other with him wherever he may go. I think today's celebration is best summarized in the following words that Lance and Stuart shared with me: 'The vows we shared 15 years ago are as meaningful today as they were at that time. We celebrate this milestone with awe, wonder, and appreciation of all who have supported us along the way. We dedicate this day to the greatest evidence of our love, our son Kalani Logan Kai-Le Chen-Hayes, and may he and all lesbian, bisexual, gay, transgender, queer, questioning and ally children and the children of lesbian, bisexual, gay and transgender parents live their lives with love, hope, courage, wisdom, playfulness, justice, and an unrelenting belief in *Everything Possible*.'"

Following the Rev. Rodriguez's opening words we read, as a couple, the poem *"I Like You"* by Sandol Stoddard Warburg. For the reading and the following two rituals, all the children present in the meetinghouse were asked to come up front and sit for the reading and then a second song, *"Everything Possible."* We chose this song to sing, as a family, because it was written for the children of LGBT parents by progressive singer-songwriter Fred Small, a heterosexual ally and Unitarian-Universalist minister in Massachusetts. It was the first song we sang to Kalani soon after being born born. Small wrote the song for a lesbian friend decades ago as a song she could sing to her nine-year-old son:

"We have cleared off the table, the leftovers saved,

Washed the dishes and put them away

I have told you a story and tucked you in tight

At the end of your knockabout day

As the moon sets its sails to carry you to sleep

Over the midnight sea

I will sing you a song no one sang to me

May it keep you good company.

You can be anybody you want to be,

You can love whomever you will

You can travel any country where your heart leads

And know I will love you still

You can live by yourself, you can gather friends around,

You can choose one special one

And the only measure of your words and your deeds

Will be the love you leave behind when you're done.

There are girls who grow up strong and bold

There are boys quiet and kind

Some race on ahead, some follow behind

Some go in their own way and time

Some women love women, some men love men

Some raise children, some never do

You can dream all the day never reaching the end

Of everything possible for you.

Don't be rattled by names, by taunts, by games

But seek out spirits true

If you give your friends the best part of yourself

They will give the same back to you.

You can be anybody you want to be,

You can love whomever you will

You can travel any country where your heart leads

And know I will love you still

You can live by yourself, you can gather friends around,

You can choose one special one

And the only measure of your words and your deeds

Will be the love you leave behind when you're done."

After the song, it was time for the "Keeper of Our Hearts" ritual designed by Kalani to celebrate his dads. Kalani walked up to each of his fathers and opened a burgundy-red heart-shaped box. Each of us was presented with a piece of dark chocolate to eat symbolizing big hearts and sweet love for each other. When the children returned to sit with their families, Rev. Rodriguez announced time for the vows and Lance and I read our original vows to each other in English and Mandarin. This time my pronunciation of

Mandarin characters, after two years of adult Sunday Chinese school classes, was easier on the ears than the original. And after the vows, there was a kiss, a pronouncement of legal husbands, and Rev. Rodriguez invited all to walk across the way to Stuyvesant Square Park for vegan cupcakes and People's Pops to celebrate our legal New York gay marriage with dessert: "As we walk over to the park please wave your rainbow flag and flaunt your feather boa"!

The impetus for the gay NYC wedding was lit at my sister's farm outside Asheville, North Carolina, where we met three new water buffalo the Spring prior when news broke that the New York State legislature had approved gay marriage starting in the summer of 2011. Since Lance was busy with online doctorate in physical therapy classes in the last two years, we had foregone our annual summer party with friends so we were overdue for a party and what better than a late summer NYC gay wedding and renewal of vows in honor of Kalani and the younger generation. Like the original ceremony, the venue was a place of worship, although that was not our original plan. But as fallen Unitarians, with a child in Quaker schools, we had become enamored of Quaker values of simplicity, anti-war, peace, and nonviolence. After checking out Manhattan's High Line urban elevated park, which was conceived and designed by a gay man, I learned that a day's rental was $50K, and with a budget one tenth of that sum, we appreciated Quaker simplicity even more at that moment and paid a small rental fee to use the 15th Street Quaker Meeting House and procured a permit for the dessert reception in adjacent Stuyvesant Square Park. Since we had survived our early summer sacred commitment ceremony/illegal wedding in Chicago with informal suits in winter fabric that made us sweat, this time we opted for tuxedos. But the choice of clothing paled in importance to the shock that finally, after a sacred commitment ceremony, a NYC domestic partnership for health benefits, a second domestic partnership for 9 more benefits in New Jersey, and a New Jersey Civil Union, we would be legally wed. New Jersey, ironically, was slower to the gay marriage scene and upon consulting with our attorney, Bill Singer, he advised us not to wait.

The legal gay wedding/15-year renewal of vows was filled with love, fun, friends, family, and the flavor of finally knowing our family had the security of legal marriage recognized in multiple (but at the time not all) USA states. The wedding was covered in two *World Journal* articles and this time, Kalani played a central role in designing the rituals.

The power of rituals in our lives has sustained our relationship and family in many ways. The importance of publicly celebrating our love and our family and renewing our vows was a playful public marker of yet another victory of love over hate that validated our LGBTQ marriage and family in the eyes of the law. And Lance cried again, just like the first one, and so did everyone else. We had a 15-year interval between events of shared love and public catharsis! I cherish and admire Lance's ability to be emotionally present. The British parts of me take a bit longer to feel my feelings in the moment, however. We had so much fun making our relationship legal, and this time we learned from the "illegal wedding," which ran over an hour with no air conditioning, to keep this one to 20 minutes. In attendance were two people from the 1997 Sacred Commitment Ceremony in Chicago, my mom, and Indiana University college friend Leigh Harbin. Also, we were honored to have attorney Bill Singer in attendance, who had assisted us with so many legal issues in creating and strengthening our family over the years. Last, we had several mixed-race gay Taiwanese/Chinese & White couple friends and their young kids present to honor all of our identities. Dessert was fun on the run--popsicles served up from an old-fashioned bicycle with an icebox from Brooklyn's local organic People's Pops, and our late lesbian friend Catherine of Catherine's Vegan Cupcakes, of Trenton, NJ, served up yummy treats and shared with us stories of growing up with a gay dad in the Village. But my favorite memory was watching a young group of bilingual Latinx children playing with the extra rainbow flags. They were having so much fun and politely asked if they could have popsicles and cupcakes and rainbow flags. YES! Who could stop city kids from celebrating? Afterward, we went back to the Highline with our photographer, San Francisco East Bay resident Al Oey, whom I had dated before I met Lance. He and Kalani bonded throughout the weekend. We could at least afford to take pictures at the High Line and a favorite one was right in front of a 5-story banner ad celebrating gay marriage. Last, we had never used the term husbands to describe ourselves until the legal wedding and since that day, we use the term with pride and ease. We realized the legal importance of using it after a decade and a half of not having full access to marriage. That weekend we traded in our New Jersey JUSTCVL license plate for HUZBNDZ. Yet even with the fun of achieving our goal of marriage equality and legal protection for our family in the USA, more equity challenges awaited our advocacy energies in Taiwan and the USA.

CHAPTER EIGHTEEN

SO MANY ISSUES, SO LITTLE TIME

USA & TAIWAN ACTIVISM

Our legal NYC gay wedding, emboldened us to increase activism on issues of social justice and equity as a family on multiple issues.

NYC MARCH ON MILLIONAIRES and BILLIONAIRES

As a school counselor educator focused on college access, I have been horrified by skyrocketing student debt and the plunge in state funding for public colleges and subsequent rise in student tuition, fees, room and board, and textbooks. CUNY's Lehman College, where I teach, is primarily students of color, poor and working class, and first-generation immigrants from Latin America, the Caribbean, West Africa, and some Asian and European-American students. CUNY appears to be a bargain for most poor and working-class undergraduates if they graduate on time with New York State grant aid (TAP), federal Pell grants, etc., but a majority of CUNY student families make less than $30K a year and have skyrocketing NYC living costs, so graduation rates remain lower than they should be. But for my graduate students seeking a master's degree in Counselor Education/School Counseling, there are few scholarships, so most take out loans and that's hard, especially as most students bring debt from undergraduate degrees, so I have seen great candidates leave because there were no funds to pay for our $22K tuition for a master's degree in school counselling (and 30 years ago CUNY tuition was free, so time to bring that back). Having watched the Occupy movement with great interest and support for challenging corporate welfare and the Wall Street bankers who engineered the 2008 recession but were never held accountable, a group of college students and others organized to challenge the debt-machinery making banks and the government wealthy at the expense of students. I decided to join in on street theater action the day of the NYC March on Millionaires/Billionaires on the Upper West Side and carried my union's "Leave No Billionaire Behind" sign. It was a festive turnout with tons of media attention and I shared my story about why I was there in the New York Daily News and with several international media outlets. In response, a few conservative bloggers challenged my remarks and attacked my academic credentials and scholarship interests. I warned my Dean the next day that folks liked to pick off progressive CUNY faculty and she said "more power to you," so that was a welcome show of support. Over time, we, as a family continued to be angry at how classism and the wealth and income gaps widened in the USA, Taiwan, and around the world. Austerity-based economics locks in people's future chances due to unfair wealth and income distribution. The march was covered both by my union's paper, the Clarion, and I had quotes in the New York Daily News:

http://www.psc-cuny.org/clarion/november-2011/labor-and-occupy-wall-street-natural-allies-0

http://www.nydailynews.com/new-york/millionaires-march-piggybacks-occupy-wall-street-momentum-protests-rage-tycoons-homes-article-1.961975

But adults were not the only ones focused on social justice advocacy in our home.

KALANI REPORTS FOR *INDYKIDS*

When I was a child, my parents bought me a subscription to *Highlights* magazine in early elementary school. I remember enjoying the stories until I outgrew them. But I wasn't much of a reader until after I finished high school. Kalani received a subscription to *Highlights* in early elementary school but it didn't last long. Kalani outgrew it faster than me. In addition, *Highlights* had begun to cover ethnic/racial diversity since the 1960s, but it hadn't discovered LGBTQ folks raising families, linguistic diversity, spiritual diversity, classism, and a host of other oppressions. I searched the internet for a regular publication focused on equity and social justice and found *IndyKids! IndyKids* is the only social justice newspaper written for and by older elementary and middle school students for elementary and middle students and older students who are learning English as a second language. Published six times a year in New York City, it has child and teen reporters from around the USA and is distributed online and in paper copies. Kalani attended a four-session youth reporter workshop and did several issues' worth of science briefs and feature articles for the paper. Kalani wrote the first *IndyKids* article reporting from Taiwan focused on three Taiwan middle school students and reported the first *IndyKids* article on what educators can do to support LGBTQ students reporting from the Supporting Students Saving Lives conference in San Diego, CA:

http://indykids.org/supporting-students-saving-lives-presenting-at-an-lgbtqia-conference-for-educators/.

LGBTQ WRITING AND ADVOCACY FOR BOYS

Our family presentation at the third Supporting Students Saving Lives conference was on issues for gay, bisexual and transgender boys and boys with LGBTQ parents. We were joined on the panel by Dr. Shari Tarver-Behring of Cal-State Northridge and her son Chuck, an out gay high school student, and Christian Burch, author of *The Manny Files* and *Hit the Road, Manny*. Kalani and I had roared in laughter when we read his books years earlier and we were excited when Christian agreed to join us to present. Earlier, Kalani and I had written letters of appreciation and inquiry to see if gay Young Adult authors whom we had read together would present with us. Alex Sanchez, author of *Bait* and the *Rainbow Boys* trilogy, wrote a gracious letter but could not attend, and we never heard back from *The Land of Stories'* Chris Colfer. (Nine months after the conference James Howe, author of *Bunnicula* and the middle grades LGBT-friendly series *The Misfits/Totally Joe/Annie On The Outside/Also Known as Elvis* sent a box of books and a letter of apology that he had received the letter but misplaced it. So instead we had brunch in New York City and talked about the power of young adult, middle grades, and elementary grade LGBTQ fiction in Kalani's life journey and in our own as gay dads in supporting our family.)

But the highlight of the conference was when award-winner Betty DeGeneres, mother of Ellen DeGeneres, saw Kalani across the way and said, "Hey young man, what are you doing here, you sure are handsome! Will you marry me?" I had stepped away when this occurred and Lance had to explain later who Betty DeGeneres was, which made it even more fun once Kalani realized her and her famous daughter's identity. Also at the conference was the NOH8 Campaign photo booth, and we took a family picture in classic white t-shirts with duct tape over our mouths and the NOH8 temporary tattoo on our faces to support for Marriage Equality and an end to LGBTQ hate:

http://www.noh8campaign.com/photo-gallery/creative-group-photos-23/photo/31064 .

THE HOMECOMING PROJECT

After the conference I had the opportunity to do the Homecoming Project with Kalani in my hometown, Park Forest, IL. When it was almost cancelled, we learned how heterosexism was rampant 3 decades after I left for college in south suburban Chicago. In preparing for my first book, *101 Solutions for School Counselors and Leaders in Challenging Times,* I compiled hundreds of resources for school counselors on eleven different oppressions:
https://lehmanedu.digication.com/stuartchen-hayes/Change_the_World.

In researching resources to challenge heterosexism, I learned about a NYC-based group called Live Out Loud (LOL) and the Homecoming Project, which asked adult LGBTQ folks to return to their high school for a presentation or lecture about life since graduation as an out LGBTQ person for a class, a GSA, or an all-school assembly. I contacted the head of the project, Tom Hernandez, who encouraged me to go as no one had returned to an Illinois high school with their group.

So, I phoned my alma mater, Rich South High School, in Richton Park, IL, and spoke to an assistant principal who was friendly but said that there were few out LGBTQ students at Rich South, and that the school was conservative. She suggested, instead, that I speak at another district high school, Rich East, where my father was school librarian and a teacher for 30 years. Since Rich East was in Park Forest, with a similar poor and working class racial/ethnic population that mirrored the shift of the far south suburbs from mostly White to mostly African-American between the early 1980s and early 2000s, I agreed.

I contacted the principal and the advisor of the Gay-Straight Alliance (GSA), and they agreed to my presenting to the GSA students. Meanwhile, I had alerted the Homecoming Project that Kalani would accompany me. On the road trip to Chicago we visited my first alma mater, Indiana University, stopped at a family of choice reunion in Chicago (Lance flew in and joined us for the weekend), and on the drive home stopped to see a lesbian classmate (and now department chair) of the Counselor Education program at Kent State, my second alma mater.

But the message I received an hour before we drove to Chicago was frustrating. The principal was cancelling the workshop due to the publicity he had received from the Homecoming Project. I had no idea what had happened, but I asked Tom to email me a copy and when I saw it the only change was that Kalani had been added on the poster, as we present as a family on LGBT issues. Tom and I saw nothing problematic about it. When I saw it, I emailed the principal that I didn't need any publicity and that it wasn't required that they post the poster. In the end, the advisor and principal conferred and agreed that I could speak but Kalani would have to remain in the principal's office (right across the hall from where Kalani's grandfather Charlie had run the library).

When we arrived at Rich East, the students were terrific. We learned that at one time the GSA had been the largest club at the school. But the community had shifted from a moderate Christian to conservative Christian atmosphere since I lived there in the '60s and '70s. In addition, after several staff in the township public schools were fired for sexually abusing students with constant bad publicity in Chicago-area media, tensions were high between staff who affirmed the GSA and community residents who felt the group was converting kids to being gay. No wonder the principal was worried about a sign that had my son's name featured on it! The last thing we wanted was to harm a supportive advisor and building leader who were allies but risking a lot in that climate simply to have me present as an adult, let alone my child. The students present were awesome—mostly African-American, a few Latinx, and one or two White students. They loved the presentation and one said, "Wow, I never realized anyone famous ever lived in this town!"

The best part was at the end when they asked questions. I asked the advisor if I could retrieve Kalani from the principal's office for the question and answer session. She said that would be fine and that the principal had agreed. The principal's secretary was very protective, however and would not release Kalani without the principal's permission. But she knocked on the door and the principal agreed.. So Kalani and I answered questions for the students—a first for them to see a mixed-race LGBTQ-headed family with one dad originating in their hometown. It was the first time we had presented in a primarily conservative Christian community and it taught an important lesson about not making assumptions about publicity in school-based workshops where community discomfort with LGBTQ issues was palpable. Yet Park Forest was not the only place we encountered heterosexism in schools. It manifested in Taiwan summer language camp in Lance's hometown of Taichung, too.

TAIWAN SUMMER MANDARIN CAMP

The next summer we were in Taichung for a couple of weeks and did some LGBTQ family presentations. Kalani encountered heterosexism at the language immersion camp from a White boy from New Zealand. There was one great ally teacher who was bilingual and noticed what was happening and handled the issue well but one traditional Taiwanese teacher didn't believe Kalani and asked him to stop lying, which was the first time we encountered educators who didn't believe Kalani at a school. At the end of the camp the bilingual teacher said thanks to us and that they had learned from our family. However, we were saddened and angered that one teacher targeted Kalani, who was the recipient of the oppression, and blamed him for being shamed.

While the language immersion camp was all international students with no Taiwanese nationals, we experienced the pull between traditional and modern Taiwan educators and were glad one teacher defended Kalani. Also during that trip, we did two Taiwan print media interviews about our family's journey through surrogacy and from no legal recognition of our relationship to gay marriage. The articles later appeared in Taiwan's _UDN (United Daily News)_ newspaper and _POTS_ magazine. We returned to the USA for a special trip celebrating Lance's birthday on the same day as a famous civil rights icon's speech and march anniversary.

MARCH ON WASHINGTON

In 2013, we attended the 50th anniversary of the March on Washington in Washington, D.C. to celebrate Martin Luther King, Jr., the civil rights movement, and Lance's birthday as he was born in Taichung on the same day as the delivery of the "I Have a Dream" speech in Washington, D.C.. Pictures of us wearing our Daddy and Papa shirts with rainbows and Kalani's rainbow shirt "I Love My Gay Dads," and quotes about our reasons for attending along with our protest sign messages landed in the _Washington Blade_ and _RGAYVA_ online magazine. Kalani hand-wrote his sign to read: "Money for Schools not Wars." Lance's sign read "Marriage Equality and Health Care For All." My sign read "Anti-War & Justice (S)Heroes and War Criminals" with a long list that followed. Kalani had the chance to hear the speakers and feel the experience of mass national anti-oppression organizing and speakers and hundreds of thousands of participants united in challenging racism, classism, war, and other oppressions:

http://www.washingtonblade.com/2013/08/24/lgbt-march-washington-participants-celebrate-king-legacy/.

We returned home to some teachable moments regarding sexuality education and preventing sexual abuse with Kalani.

SEXUALITY EDUCATION WITH KALANI

We decided from before Kalani was born that it was important for Kalani have askable dads regarding sexuality education. It meant scouring the picture and chapter book lists for books with diverse families, same-gender parents, and LGBT youth--a small but growing list. It meant finding child-friendly resources on sexuality education although none completely covered the same-gender family waterfront. We listened carefully as Kalani went through childhood, late childhood, and early adolescence. In elementary and middle school, Kalani's classmates (and sometimes teachers) found Kalani the askable child regarding sexuality issues. At times that wasn't fun because Kalani didn't want to be in that role when teachers didn't know an answer or when Kalani was put on the spot by younger classmates. However, we were proud that fall when the local peer health LGBTQ teen group came to Kalani's middle school and Kalani had all of the accurate answers for their questions. The peer educators loved it and Kalani had the chance to share knowledge and be affirmed inside and outside the school.

When we have presented as a family, Kalani has often been asked questions by adults, and Kalani has a sharp wit and is able think on his feet in public and school settings regarding sexuality issues. We made sure Kalani knew appropriate names for body parts for various genders from early on. We talked about puberty and changes to be expected long before they occurred. When it was time to talk about sexual abuse, Kalani had the chance to hear a lecture from me or read novels. Kalani chose to read Toni Morrison's *The Bluest Eye* and later Alex Sanchez's *Bait*. *The Bluest Eye* deals with incest/sexual abuse, sexism, racism and sexual abuse toward a girl, and *Bait* is focused on issues of sexual abuse toward a Latinx youth and deals with heterosexism, questioning identity, and the healing process after abuse. Our discussions with both books were rich and helped Kalani look at the intersectionality of characters and our similar and different experiences of oppressions as a mixed-race, bilingual, dual-national gay-dad family. Kalani's coming out as gay to the whole middle school, and Kalani's part in family media interviews and presentations on LGBTQ issues in Taiwan and the USA evidenced a level of maturity, confidence, and clarity that made us proud as dads. Another presentation occurred on Asian/Pacific Islander LGBTQ family issues in Boston the following year on the way to Kalani's first stay-away camp experience in New Hampshire.

MODERN FAMILY: LGBTQ PARENTING, YOUTH, & HEALTH IN ASIAN-AMERICAN COMMUNITIES

Lance was contacted by the Taiwan student associations at MIT and Harvard to participate in an Asian-American LGBTQ family health conference. We shared our story as gay dads for a large audience in Cambridge, MA en route to Kalani's stay-away summer camp:
 http://sampan.org/2014/06/wemeet-series-modern-family-lgbt-parenting-youth-and-health-in-asian-american-communities/ .

Since Kalani was almost 11, it was time to try a sleep-away summer camp. One of the unusual aspects of Kalani's middle school was an annual 3-day camping trip for teachers, students, and families during the school year and Kalani loved being in the woods and the outdoors. Kalani enjoyed camp the most when we allowed him to go without us under the supervision of a classmate's parents. Like Kalani's first overnight leadership trip with his classmates a prior year in Williamsburg, VA, when asked the best part of each Kalani replied, "Being away from parents!" While some oclassmates clung to their parents teary-eyed at leaving home, not Kalani. We set limits and boundaries and Kalani was ready for more independence. So we let Kalani choose where to do summer camp. As the child of gay dads, we gave options including camps catering to LGBTQ kids and kids with LGBTQ parents. Kalani chose a Harbor camp in New Hampshire for LGBTQ families and non-binary/transgender/questioning/ally youth.

After that decision, we decided that for the first time in a decade that Lance and I should have a week to ourselves for vacation. We'd taken long weekends over the years but never had the luxury of a full week alone as a couple since Kalani was born. We drove to Montreal and enjoyed a week at the Jazz festival spending time sightseeing and eating our way through Montreal and the Gay Village. We enjoyed traditional French cuisine and a fantastic Taiwanese tea café, Nos Thes (Our Teas) in the gay village. We tea was as good as any we had sampled outside of Taiwan the food authentic..

We talked to the two cute men working behind the counter and learned one was the co-owner with his sister. Upon daily discussions over tea and food we met his mom, who assisted with the shop's two locations. Upon sharing our story as gay parents of Kalani, she shared that her daughter, the co-owner, was a lesbian with a partner. Her mom was a strong ally for the LGBTQ community in Montreal, especially considering her husband was a Christian minister. By sharing our story and how Kalani came into our life, she shared that she'd never really talked with her daughter much about her being lesbian and that it was time having heard about our story. She said we'd always be welcome to stay with her in future travels to Montreal. We were grateful and amazed at our new Taiwanese LGBTQ connections in francophone Montreal. Soon after we turned to the USA, we focused on climate justice advocacy.

CLIMATE CHANGE MARCH

Even though we have owned five hybrid cars (an electric will be the last, and then it's public transit after that), put solar panels on the house (or bought all green energy from electric suppliers), and are recycling experts, we hadn't done enough for climate justice. So, when the first People's Climate March (2014) was announced, we marched with the PSC/CUNY union in NYC. We wore our "More Love Less Capitalism" shirts from Syracuse Cultural Workers and enjoyed the camaraderie of 400,000+ folks protesting the visit of world leaders to the United Nations not acting fast enough to pressure corporations and governments to end the use of fossil fuels and reverse human-made climate change.

Soon afterward, *Next Magazine* sent a film crew from Taiwan to our home for the weekend reporting in digital print and digital video segments about our family, including a separate article on Kalani's Aunt Alison and her reasons to pursue surrogacy:

http://www.nextmag.com.tw/magazine/people/20141022/9555112

http://www.nextmag.com.tw/breaking-news/people/20141023/9634443

In addition to climate justice,, we advocated on mixed-race identity issues.

CONFRONTING MIXED-RACE ISSUES & RACISM:

Kalani had some mixed-race peers at school and with some of our friends. Kalani knew from an early age how to name specific nationalities and ethnicities (Taiwanese (Han), Scottish, English) and racial identities (Asian, White, Mixed-Race). Growing up Kalani did not have to deal overtly with others' comments about his looks from other children although many adults over the years described his look as physically attractive. Kalani learned to question, however, whether those comments were exoticizing or genuine--not always easy to discern. But one incident in middle school was painful when Kalani encountered anti-Asian bias from a mixed-race student of African and European descent. As parents we tried to downplay the external and help Kalani focus on the internal as what is most important in people. But in a social-media obsessed world, it's easier to say that than have to negotiate it as a middle schooler.

However, as Kalani's monoracial dads, we never had the experience growing up as mixed race. We gently accepted compliments and shuddered when we heard "mixed-race Asian and White kids are the cutest." We don't see his Kalani's look as better or worse than others. Kalani is old enough as an adolescent to see how others' views more accurately and calls out the racism and heterosexism that targets Asian males as less attractive or not sexy.

When a mixed-race classmate kept trying to box Kalani into stereotypical Asian images, Kalani was angry. She didn't understand the size of eyes is similar worldwide but the difference is some Asians have an eyelid with an epicanthic fold. Teachers at Kalani's middle school raised issues of racism and anti-Asian bias in the USA in history and visual literacy classes, but it was painful to be a personal target from another mixed-race student knowing the history of how Asians have been persecuted, harassed and discriminated against in the USA. We made sure Kalani knew the history of anti-Asian oppression in the USA including Chinese men abused as they built the Western half of the transcontinental railroad, exclusionary immigration policies (both in the past and current), limitations on work and housing, yellow peril, Japanese concentration camps, model minority stereotypes, Muslim-bashing, Arab- and Iranian-bashing), and how Asians are still persecuted and ostracized in the USA.

In response, Kalani chose to do a major middle school paper on the mixed-race experience as a mixed-race person to be stronger in challenging racism and biases toward mixed-race people. But challenging racism wasn't enough. We returned to Taiwan for a series of public presentations challenging Taiwan's refusal of gay marriage and surrogacy using our family's narrative and evidence-based research.

FIGHTING FOR MARRIAGE EQUALITY AND SURROGACY IN TAIWAN

For years Lance advocated tirelessly on Facebook for LGBTQ rights in the USA and Taiwan. He became an early member of the LGBTQ Family Association of Taiwan and helped organize events, and we have spoken as a family at numerous events supporting them. Lance has been friends with gay erotic novelist Yousheng Hsu and his husband Gray Harriman, the first gay couple married by the mayor of Taipei. He is also close with Joe Zhou, who is a counseling psychologist in Taipei and an expert on the use of narrative counseling theory to affirm LGBTQ persons..

Lance arranged for us to speak in front of LaLaMoms, the first lesbian mom and wannabe mom group in Taiwan.. In 2015, we did five public speaking appearances in Taiwan about our family's journey and the importance of marriage equality and surrogacy in Taiwan. Lance presented in Mandarin and Kalani and I answered questions in English with Mandarin translation. We had standing-room-only audiences for each presentation of between 50 and 200 persons and lively question and answer sessions. Each time we presented, more people became affirming about the need for both marriage equality and surrogacy legislation in Taiwan. The locations of our presentations were:

— National Pingtung University,
— TaKao Bookstore, Kaohsiung,
— Kaohsiung Medical University (KMU),

– Shih Chien University, Taipei, and
– National Changhua University of Education (NCUE).

The following year, in April of 2016, on my second sabbatical, I guest lectured at NCUE, KMU, & Shih Chien University on LGBTQ counseling over the lifespan. I also did an Unlearning Oppression workshop while teaching a spring semester school counseling course at Shih Chien University. Upon my return to the USA, we were interviewed as a family for the first Japanese-language book on gay parenting.

Our work in schools and communities to educate about our family and LGBTQ issues in two countries is exemplified in the fight for LGBTQ inclusion in Kalani's elementary/middle school, a slow seemingly intractable battle.

CHAPTER NINETEEN

MIDDLE SCHOOL MAYHEM & BEYOND

Our quest for LGBT advocacy at Kalani's elementary/middle school was never-ending. After five years, Princeton Friends School finally hung a rainbow pride flag that we donated in the school gym alongside international flags representing the countries of origin of students and staff. After years of asking, we were told by the head of school at the time, "We're not a Quaker Meeting we're a Quaker School," implying that activism occurred in Meeting but not at school.

I did a LGBT 101 presentation for some students at the school on two different occasions for their social justice day and once did an Unlearning Oppression training for the staff, the first time they received multicultural staff development in three decades of operation. Over the years Kalani distributed GLSEN's Safe Space Stickers, and two students came out to me at a presentation. When Kalani was in seventh grade, a straight male teacher taught the book *Two Boys Kissing,* and Kalani came out to classmates during the discussion. The teacher said it was one of the most moving movements in his career as a teacher.

Most teachers were fine but we had systemic disappointments. We had hoped the school would be anti-oppression but we learned otherwise (and we had been warned by current parents of color wary that it had a reputation of senior administrator intransigence). The most upsetting incident was when a teacher attacked our parenting style in an email to school administrators. We found out because she accidentally sent it to us (karma via technology).

When I read it and realized what had happened I simply replied,, "Was this meant for me?" and copied Lance. We then talked by phone and talked about how inappropriate this was and how we would respond if apologies came through. We received quasi-apologies (multiple paragraphs beating around the bush versus a simple I'm sorry) emailed from the teacher and the head of school within 24 hours, and then it was ignored until we asked for a formal meeting to discuss the issue months later. When we arrived at the meeting, the head of school refused to talk about it. We had had our challenges with that person's leadership over the years and whatever trust and credibility was left disappeared at that moment. Kalani later heard that same teacher referring to HIV/AIDS as a disease only gay people get. Kalani challenged it on the spot. In 2017 we learned that teacher was fired.

Another teacher attempted to teach about LGBTIQ issues in one of Kalani's classes but didn't know what the I or Q stood for when questioned. The students asked Kalani, who shared what Intersex and Queer/Questioning meant with the class. In history class, when the students struggled with the word *suffrage*, Kalani shared this sentence with the class: "Students deserve suffrage so that we can vote for a GSA at PFS!"

Again, the head of school refused the students petitioning for a GSA with no ability to say why other than she, a White woman, opposed "affinity groups." As a fan of public schools, I resented paying tuition at an independent school that refused to create a GSA, something a public school in the USA, by law, must support if students request one. By this time, Taiwan had passed Gender/Sexuality Education laws as well ensuring public school student K-12 received comprehensive sexuality and gender education including LGBTA Issues.

At this point, most of the families in Kalani's cohort had great anger toward the school leadership on multiple issues. We put our energy into searching for a strong high school that would better support and challenge Kalani's talents, spirit, and cultural identities.

Kalani was aware of the challenges at this school as a student frustrated by a lack of responsiveness and change when students brought legitimate concerns to teachers and administrators. We followed Kalani's lead and backed away from further confrontations with administration as Kalani was doing admirably without our interventions. Watching and hearing Kalani's voice as an activist emerge was exciting. Kalani became passionate challenging ageism from some teachers and administrators to ensure children and youth had a greater voice in the world let alone at PFS. There was no better example of Kalani's courage and wisdom than his 8th grade graduation speech.

An annual PFS tradition, each of the 14 members of the 8th grade graduating class of 2016 were asked to write a speech to deliver to the entire school community at commencement. Each speech was thoroughly reviewed and vetted by advisors and English teachers. Kalani created two versions, however, with our permission; one that was vetted and one that was the truth. At the last minute on the podium, Kalani pulled out from his pocket the real speech and read from it as the head of school clutched her chest and the other administrator and his advisor mouthed words with looks of shock and panic. Kalani's gentle, funny, powerful critique of a school whose administration often did not listen to students' voices wafted over the hundreds of family members gathered under a White canopy. Kalani spoke these words with hair gelled back wearing a bow tie from a podium on the steps of the original Friends Meeting House surrounded by tall trees, chirping birds, sweet spring floral scents, and a Revolutionary War-era cemetery:

"All through my life as far as I can remember I have been in school: from pre-school in Taiwan to a Mandarin Immersion elementary school to PFS. I found school enjoyable until 7th grade when I started to see many cracks and faults in the educational systems within which I had grown up. I found that education and frustration seemed to go hand in hand whether it was homework (which admittedly was my responsibility) or the school administration's inability to listen to kids' wants and needs. Through my years at PFS my favorite subjects have been science, then a small tad later art, then later science, until about two years ago when it went back to art. I have a lot of gratitude and wish to thank the teachers in whose classes I've thrived, especially some art teachers both at PFS and outside PFS: (I am not allowed to name one of these teachers because of the rules for departing remarks, but you know who you are if you're here, my dance teachers for nine years at Princeton Ballet School, and my piano teacher of six years Fang-Ting Liu), most of my advisors (one for organization, one for writing, and one for help with all of it and more, once again I'm not allowed to name names so you know who you are), and a science teacher (still not allowed to name names).

In my science career I had been interested in biology for a short time, robotics, physics and the many trinkets of Brian's ginormous desk (I can say that name, right?...because no one's feelings would get hurt. Right?). In my arts career I have always been interested in singing and dancing, musical theatre, and more recently sketching and stenciling. I could never have guessed as a small child that I would be where I am today: Standing here in eighth grade speaking. I have grown over the years in some ways better than others, having picked up a collection of different traits from different people.

If I had to pick one quote to sum up certain experiences in my school life it would be: "Life, Liberty, and the Pursuit of Happiness: we fought for these ideals we shouldn't settle for less." -Thomas Jefferson as quoted from the musical *Hamilton*. I definitely agree with this quote as I have always found all three important. Ironically, the real Thomas Jefferson did not let many people have those ideals as he was a slave owner.

One thing that many people will disagree with me about is bullying incidents at PFS. I feel that many people don't believe this as PFS is presented as such a safe place. Even recently I was shocked to find that only a small group of my cohort was aware of such incidents. I personally am aware that there have been several incidents that have occurred but it's not my place to disclose any of that. Anywho I guess what I'm trying to say is that there have been ups and downs, I feel that I have moved past this stage of my life and I am certain that I am at least all but big toe out the door.

But I would like to take a moment to ask that any teachers listening to remember that it does not mean that you shouldn't listen to kids' suggestions just because you think that it is their way of being ready to leave the nest (really from my experience they just have more of a middle ground between adult and child understanding of what should be happening to make improvements). Bye!"

Afterward, Kalani was mobbed by classmates who admired the courage it took to be the only student to honestly speak truth to power in a speech. One of the straight boys said Kalani had more balls than all the other boys put together. Havign enrolled at George School in Newtown, PA, a Quaker high school, Kalani was the only freshman to address the annual school-wide LGBT assembly held in October 2016. Kalani shared the story of growing up in a two-dad gay family. Soon afterward, older students on the student council invited Kalani to be one of two freshmen on the campus Heteronormativity Task Force. Kalani joined Open Doors, the school GSA, and other clubs. Kalani has been a source of great learning for us as parents. But wise old souls in youthful bodies deserve surprises, and we developed a unique ritual to honor Kalani's 13th birthday.

CHAPTER TWENTY

THE FIRST GAY TEEN DAY RITUAL

It was an unusual start to a birthday because for prior birthday celebrations we always had discussions with Kalani about where to go, what to do, and who to invite. Not this time. All we said was be ready by 11:00 a.m. At 11:00 a.m. the doorbell rang and two of Kalani's middle school classmates, Emma Johnson and Nina Bergman, were at the door along with Nina's parents, Andrea and Eric. They told Kalani they were going out to lunch in Princeton to celebrate his 13th birthday. They didn't tell Kalani what the rest of the day had in store. While Kalani was eating lunch, we jumped in the car and headed east to Asbury Park, New Jersey.

At the end of lunch, Kalani and friends got in Eric and Andrea's car and said there was more to come but Kalani had to wear a blindfold. But on the way, they received a call from Lance stating that guests from New York City were in slow traffic on the Garden State Parkway and that the surprise needed to be delayed. So they stopped at LGBTQ- & ally-owned Words Bookstore on Cookman St., and Kalani was un-blindfolded and recognized the premises. Co-owner Jan presented Kalani with a gift certificate for books. Then Kalani was blindfolded again and taken to the north side of Asbury. When the blindfold was removed, it took Kalani a few seconds to realize he was now in front of the new Asbury Hotel. Kalani was led in the door and saw some folks he didn't recognize including a video crew and a photographer taking pictures—like personal paparazzi. The event space was tall and beckoning and then Kalani saw me and heard my voice over the loudspeaker saying, "Kalani, come on in, we're all waiting for you. Welcome to your First Gay Teen Day celebration!"

Kalani entered the room noticing floor-to ceiling windows, a variety of seating options including four large bean-bag chairs (including a red one, his favorite), and Kalani was asked to sit in front of a table with both of his fathers on either side under a huge arched spray of rainbow balloons. Emma sat on a bean-bag chair to the right and Nina sat on a bean-bag chair to his left. Kalani looked stunned and unsure of what was happening. (Originally we had been booked in the fifth-floor ourdoor sky beach lounge on artificial turf overlooking the shore but with 108 degree heat in the full sun that day, the hotel staff said it safer to move to the air-conditioned indoor event space).

I then said,

"Surprise, Kalani! Before we begin, we want to thank the staff of The Asbury Hotel who have gone above and beyond five floors up in the sky overlooking the Atlantic Ocean and boardwalk for this gay coming of age ritual and birthday celebration. The manager of the hotel, Larry, and staff Connor and Suzanne were attentive, affirming, and terrific to work with. They agreed with us on the importance of creating a coming of age ritual for a gay teen and have landed a few triple twists along the way. But most of all we thank the citizens of Asbury Park, NJ, a town that is LGBTQ-affirming, welcoming of people of color, and celebrates local arts, local cuisine, and local gay-owned businesses. Last, we want to thank Mr. Richard Koob, Dr. Erin Mason, and Dr. Shari Tarver-Behring who were unable to be here in person today and who all made donations to GLSEN to support LGBT youth in schools in Kalani's honor. We start with a Wiccan ritual honoring Kalani's spiritual tradition, share spoken words on this first day of your journey as a gay teen, and then dessert and dancing or mingling to music here on your lucky 13th birthday."

The ritual began with an introduction:

"To honor Kalani's Wiccan tradition, we co-create a ritual with closest friends and neighbors. Assisting us are the other teens and their families--Emma Johnson, Nina and the Bergmans, Penzi Hill, and Emma, Hanna, and the Gampper family. So everyone ready? We'll call the directions and watch and listen carefully.

We thank you for this day and the chance to celebrate the life of Kalani Chen-Hayes and friends and family. We cast a circle and seek to raise energy for the ritual and celebration by calling the directions and celebrating the elements that give us life and nourish our spirits on the Earth. We start with calling on the elements from the direction of the East--air, and spirit symbolized with the color yellow and the Sun. We next call on the elements of the direction of the West--expansive calming BLUE water here near the great Atlantic Ocean. We next call on the elements of the North--giving thanks to our Mother and drumming to the heartbeat of the great GREEN Earth. Last, we call on the elements of the last direction, the South, Fire, with the color RED representing passion and dance. May you surround Kalani and all gathered here today with sustenance, protection, and creative energy!"

As each element was called, Kalani's close friends and neighbors shared their messages from the front of the room---some verbal and some nonverbal--honoring each of the elements. After the last element, I stated,

"We end the ritual by releasing and thanking the elements. You are released and thank you Fire from the Direction of the South, You are released and thank you Mother Earth from the Direction of the North, You are released and thank you Water from the direction of the West and you are released and thank you Air/Spirit from the direction of the East. Blessed be and brightest blessings to all!"

The next portion of the ceremony was having 30 LGBTQ persons and allies close to Kalani and our family share messages of greetings and empowerment upon entering the LGBTQ community as a teen at age 13. For those friends and family who were not able to attend, Lance and I alternated reading the messages (See Appendix C).

With 30 messages read, it was time for singing happy birthday in English, Mandarin, and Spanish, and as dessert was rolled out I said:

"And now, dessert, let's sing three birthday songs to Kalani--English, Mandarin, and Spanish, while we await the following delicious surprise: 48 birthday donuts from gay- and ally-owned Asbury Park's Purple Glaze Donuts: 2 dozen assorted (Triple Chocolate, Mango Tango, Strawberry Shortcake, Key Lime), 1 dozen Gay Pride, 1 dozen mixed Broadway (Phantom, Wicked, Book of Mormon, Les Miz, Hamilton, and Dr. Who), and 4 Vegan donuts. Baba Lance will light the candles on the donut of Kalani's choice and Kalani will make a wish and blow out the candles as a mixtape of Kalani's favorite songs curated by Baba Lance plays. Please join us for dancing and schmoozing afterward here and in the lobby of the hotel."

Kalani chose the Les Miz donut and ended up with a bright-red tongue from the icing. Then, Kalani, who had appeared a bit uncomfortable during the ceremony, ran to find a bathroom since there had been no bathroom break all day.

Sometime in 2014 I mentioned to Lance it would be fun to create a ritual for Kalani's 13th birthday as a coming of age celebration to honor the passage out of childhood and toward adulthood in the teenage years. Lance thought it was a great idea. There is no coming of age ceremony in LGBTQ culture for teens, let alone children entering the teenage years. We've watched adult LGBTQ folks reclaim the high school prom ritual, we have pride parades for all ages, and we see more picture and chapter books written about LGBTQ children and adolescents. Yet, many world cultures do a formal community ritual to bring children into adolescence and adulthood such as bar and bat mitzvahs, vision quests, quinceaneras.

With my training as a family counsellor, I was influenced by the work of Evan Imber-Black on the power of rituals in maintaining and strengthening couples and families. We've been intentional as a couple with Lance's regular home-cooked meals evenings and weekends, regular trips to Taiwan, annual gatherings of friends and family for an annual summer party, sacred commitment ceremony, domestic partnerships, a civil union, and legal gay marriage. For Kalani, we did the traditional Man Yue (first month celebration in Chinese culture) ceremony and have always had a fun birthday party to mark each year of passage (be it a request for Sushi at age 2 to an Escape The Room party with friends in NYC). Yet we wanted something unique to welcome Kalani into the LGBTQ community celebrating mutiple identities.

When we told friends our secret plan, everyone was supportive and excited. No one had heard of something like this for a gay teen. For us and our LGBTQ friends, this was more than a birthday party for Kalani. It symbolized how far we have come as a community of LGBTQ singles, couples, and families that we have the ability to pass on our hopes, dreams, inspiration, whimsy, fabulosity, and shared struggle to the next generation with a coming of age ceremony.

It took 12 months of planning (sabbatical helped) to create and stage the ritual. The first part involved where would we hold it. That was easy. Asbury Park has served as our gay spirit home since we moved to NYC metro in 1998. We've sung there with New Jersey Gay Men's chorus, enjoyed the beach, attended many a film at the independent art house owned by two film-makers: The Showroom, and had many great meals, desserts, and day trips to the beach over two decades.

Next was finding a venue. The Asbury Hotel had recently opened and we figured it would be fun and queer-friendly. When the gay manager, Larry Dembrun, heard about our story and the event,, he said that the hotel would pay for it because he and the staff were moved by Kalani's family story and the importance a coming of age ritual for a gay teen. We originally planned to be on the outdoor roof deck "sky beach" overlooking the ocean, but the day of the event it was 99 degrees with heat warnings making it feel like 110 so the staff put us in their indoor space so that we and the dessert didn't melt.

Next was what to do for dessert. Mom and gay son (Jacki and Wesley) co-owned locally-sourced donut shop, Purple Glaze, was the only option considered. They have taken Asbury by sugar storm having previously surprised Kalani with their Star Wars and gay rainbow donuts.. We also wanted a rainbow balloon arch and to focus the ritual on Kalani's Wiccan spirituality. So, I called a friend skilled in both--Joe Kaufman and husband Mark Brimhall-Vargas had hosted us a couple of times when we traveled to Washington, D. C. Joe intuited about Kalani being gay when he met Kalani at age 2. As long-time husbands and Wiccans, and with Joe a balloon artist, he was the perfect consultant. We had hoped that they could join us in person but as dads of a large aviary having recently moved to Massachusetts they were in search of a bird-keeper to watch the flock and could not attend. So, Joe was most helpful on how to do a Wiccan ritual. Joe suggested not only calling the four directions but to allow the guests to be spontaneous in how they created and interpreted the elements: air, water, fire, and earth. We asked the four teens and their family members present to take one element each, so Nina Bergman and her family presented water, Emma and Hanna Gampper and her parents presented fire, Emma Johnson presented earth and Penzi Hill presented spirit. We found a local balloon artist to create the rainbow arch.

The last element was to record the day for posterity in photos and videos and we hired Dan Gramkee of New Hope, PA and his husband Scott Kleinbart assisted as both were excited about a teen gay coming of age ritual and recording it. Dan and Scott helped us scheme about what the day would be like. In addition, the daughter of a neighbor in Newtown, PA introduced us to a friend working with lesbian filmmaker, media artist, and mom Laura Zaleya, a professor at Temple University in Philadelphia. Her team was producing the first internet-based interactive documentary on LGBTQ families and LGBTQ family creation and wondered if we would consider being filmed. We invited her team to attend the ritual and film the before and after portions with guests. She and her intern Jake and his boyfriend Sebastian wrote a wonderful message for the ritual about how touched and inspired they had been with Kalani's story and filming our family. The documentary, including footage from the day of the ritual, is online at:

https://lgbtq-family.com/ (background and how interactive documentary works)
https://video.helloeko.com/v/MwokGM (the documentary)

Next up was finalizing the guest list and one last item. Prior to the arrival of the donuts and after the Wiccan ritual, we wanted to have personal messages delivered to Kalani by attendees. Realizing that folks in Taiwan and at long distances in the USA would not be attending, Lance and I agreed to read messages for folks unable to be in person. Lance compiled all of the written messages into a keepsake book for Kalani to remember the day by. In the end, we invited 80 persons plus hotel staff who shared the event with us with 30 messages delivered to Kalani.

After the ritual, we spent hours talking with friends. Kalani then was surprised with pizza on the town with friends at Talula's. Next, Kalani was surprised with his first Asbury Park ghost tour starting at Paranormal Books and then a final surprise--overnighting at the Asbury Hotel.

In reflecting on the day, Kalani was in shock and somewhat embarrassed as an introvert. Kalani loved the donuts and the surprises but didn't know all of the persons sharing messages so that felt a bit awkward at times. But Kalani was gracious and handled it well. The folks who were most appreciative in the moment were the adults and other teens in the room. There was not a dry eye in the house and several speakers were visibly overcome with emotion during the event (including Lance).

For older members of the LGBTQ community, the ability to create rituals that affirm the next LGBTQ generation reminds us of how far we have come as a movement. None of us had anything like a First Gay Teen Day in our journeys. Most of us came out in times of great fear and danger for our physical safety well into adulthood. The tears of joy on faces were tears of gratitude for the many victories our community has made as well as the losses along the way. We know there is much more to do.

The power of co-creating ritual is that you don't know how it will turn out nor how people will be affected by it. But in a world that still has too much hate, this was a celebration of love. Most LGBTQ youth are not raised by LGBTQ parents. If other families can recreate this type of ritual, it is the chance for parents and guardians, families of origin, and families of choice to welcome LGBTQ children/teens into their future surrounded by supportive community. It also allowed adults, whose coming out journeys were often more difficult and dangerous, a delicious moment to celebrate a 2-generation gay family (although we believe it's 3- and 4- generation on both sides of our family based on intuition, family stories, and queering our family's history/herstory). The joy of the celebration led us to reflect on our next steps as a couple and family.

CHAPTER TWENTY-ONE

USA STRUGGLE

We had little warning that just a few months after the 13th birthday party ritual for Kalani that USA political dynamics would turn upside-down with the electoral college (but loss of the popular vote by 3 million) victory of President #45. Nothing like starting a presidency with a wacky initial phone call to Taiwan President Tsai Ing-Wen elevating Taiwan briefly only to have him mercurially dump Taiwan in favor of China weeks later.

Our USA and Taiwan activism entered a new phase after the most expensive USA presidential election. So much money misspent by two corrupt, unethical, corporate-funded parties that ignored average voters and major issues facing the USA and the world and instead focused on the desires of their billionaire backers and the corporate media they finance to do their bidding under the illusion of democracy.

Our reality, like most others in the USA, is living in an oligarchy run by billionaires. Their desires trample on the needs of all but the wealthiest in an increasingly unequal society based on record corporate CEO pay and profits, corporate welfare, and a decades-long decline in real wages for all but the wealthiest workers. Families of color have the least wealth and the housing collapse of the last decade decimated the savings and net worth of most families of color.

Ever since the 2015-16 USA presidential campaign, the USA was filled with heated rhetoric, hate, the re-emergence of White nationalism, and a series of well-publicized attacks on persons of color, LGBTQ folks, women, persons with disabilities, immigrants, poor and working class persons, and persons of nondominant faith traditions (especially Muslims). Attacks by the most right-wing conservative political and religious elements continued at the legislative, judicial, and executive branches of government. #45, in the final days of the campaign, appeared a block from our home at a final campaign rally.

That event sent Kalani and a large group of high school friends and students from other high schools out to protest with many adults in the community. I went all around the outskirts posting Jill Stein/Ajamu Baraka for President/Vice President signs so that the attendees would be greeted by a progressive alternative on their way out the door. Lance, my mom, and I registered as Greens when we moved to Pennsylvania as we wanted to challenge the corruption of both parties (neoliberal and neoconservative) by billionaire and PAC-money financing as a direct threat to democracy. We voted for ecology, grassroots democracy, peace, and social justice with a belief in building a multi-party democracy no longer under the influence of corporate cash and billionaires was the way forward.

The issues of voting justice became central to our concerns about living in the USA. The amount of voter suppression done by one party and barely contested by the other party (which has also engaged in it locally in

Philadelphia), added to our support for the Green Party, which refuses corporate contributions and focuses on an eco-socialist approach to politics.

Corporations have too much power and influence and are harming people and the planet. I helped revitalize the Bucks County Green Party in 2016 by helping run Green candidates locally and organizing the two colleges in the county for Greens through our presence at voter registration drives. Our family was part of the 2016 presidential recount effort in Pennsylvania, having secured the necessary affidavit with a notary and paid the $50 fee at the county courthouse.

After learning how outdated and inappropriate Pennsylvania's recount laws were, I attended a national Green Party-sponsored seminar in voting justice and decided to make a difference locally. I attended the Green Party attempt to open the debates on Long Island in the fall, the poor people's march in Philadelphia, a rally by Greens at the time of the Democratic National Convention, a Green pre-election rally with Lance and Kalani in Philadelphia, and our family attended Occupy Inauguration with Dr. Jill Stein in Washington, D.C. I was invited to keynote the Green Party of Pennsylvania convention with a speech entitled "Growing the Green Wave in our Own Backyards: Joy and Purpose in Challenging Neoliberalism and Fascism."

But attending rallies and giving a keynote speech were not enough. I ran for Judge of Elections in Newtown Township as a Green, unopposed, and was elected to public office in November of 2017 for a four-year term. I was then elected as both a Green Party of Pennsylvania delegate and a Green Party of the United States National Committee Delegate working on the platform committee. I championed better educational justice language, sex worker advocacy language, and Modern Monetary Theory in platform changes, and, although not always successful, vowed to continue advocacy in future years. I was thrilled in 2018 when it was announced that the recount lawsuit brought by Dr. Jill Stein in Pennsylvania was successful and that secure, verifiable, auditable paper ballots were now mandated for the entire state of Pennsylvania, and worked with local Bucks County group Save Bucks Votes to ensure their successful roll out..

I will never forget days after the 2016 presidential election, Lance awakened and shared that he felt scared and unsafe to be in a mostly White suburb after spending his whole life in cities or majority-Asian suburbs. He said he didn't know for sure which White people he could trust.

After two traffic tickets he was also tired of driving while Asian. My White privilege meant I could speed or blow a red light or stop signs in a White town and be less likely to get a ticket. We were not the only ones to lose a lot of sleep after the election aftermath from the classism, racism, sexism, genderism, ableism, heterosexism, religionism, and immigrationism emanating from the new presidential administration, White Nationalists, and the billionaire class in charge of USA politics.

I watched independent media (*Democracy Now!*, the *Intercept*, and *Jacobin* magazine) regularly and followed activists, writers, and artists on Twitter. I focused on local activism--such as No DAPL and No Pipeline protests bi-weekly in Newtown and weekly #FridaysWithFitzpatrick protests at our newly elected local congressperson's office, Republican Representative Brian Fitzpatrick, 1.5 miles away from home and across the street from Kalani's high school. Bucks County was one of the few competitive congressional races in the USA as the county has about even registrations for both of the corporate-funded political parties. Both congressional candidates had millions of dollars in outside funding pour into the county with the Republicans having spent the most of the two parties and that funding won. Since I also ran the Bucks County Green Party Twitter feed, I had the chance to use Twitter for online protests and regularly questioning legislative priorities, a lack of communication or Town Hall meetings with constituents, and radio silence (or lip service) on issues of ecology, grassroots democracy, peace, and social justice.

As #45's administration and Republicans continued to attack all nondominant groups, we became more visible as a family with LGBTQ activism in the USA and Taiwan. Prior to the 2016 election, we presented at the last Reach Higher/White House School Counseling and College Access conference in Washington, D.C. on what school and college access counselors need to know to support LGBTQ youth and families. We were also interviewed for SET News TV Ch. 12 in Hoboken, NJ on marriage equality in Taiwan and on our relationship as a couple : https://www.youtube.com/watch?v=M7rfRjPLGpY&feature=youtu.be.

We attempted to attend the women's march in Washington, D.C., but we were blocked from the Metro by a jam of 10,000 people attempting to enter at the last stop of the line. We took our posters, "Fight Ugliness with Fabulosity" and "Strong Men Honor Women and Their Vulvas" and cheered on the masses attempting to get to the march and then headed north to Philly to catch the remnants of the Philly march. Our black on pink posters now hang in my office windows in the Bronx at Lehman College overlooking the Goulden Avenue reservoir.

In addition to being allies for women's rights, I wrote a speech at our first Lehman College campus Immigration SpeakOut co-sponsored by our student government and our reinvigorated activist campus union chapter of the PSC-CUNY (Professional Staff Congress) in the fall of 2016 after the election. With a dual-national family and a house full of recent immigrants including Green-card holders from Taiwan, I encouraged my mostly first-generation immigrant students and colleagues to organize and fight against deportations, raids, travel bans, walls, and immigrationism rooted in White supremacy in the Bronx and across the USA.

RACIST INCIDENTS AND ANTI-RACISM RALLY

As the GOP continued to spew hate and White supremacy in the USA, Lance and Kalani felt increasingly targeted as persons of color living in a primarily White eastern Pennsylvania suburb. Although our development and the one next to it had a substantial percentage of Asians, primarily South Asians and Koreans, 90% of Bucks County was White and often felt unwelcoming to our family having lived in the more racially diverse areas of New Jersey and in Taiwan.

Lance was targeted for eating while Asian as well in Newtown, PA. We were at my birthday dinner at Boccaccio's, an Italian restaurant, and watched as the White owner spent a great deal of time chatting at each table with guests--all White--and Kalani and Lance both watched his progress moving around the room. But he didn't linger at our table of all Asians (my brother and sister-in law Chun and Gloria, their son Ray, Kalani, and Lance) and me and my mom. The owner addressed me quickly with his eyes down and asked how was our food as he walked off without even waiting for my response. It was a painful, classic micro-aggression that our table of mostly Asians were not welcomed in his restaurant (we soon after tried the newly opened Acqua e Farina in Newtown, with a most gracious hostess/manager and have become regulars).

Right about that time Lance was stopped for a traffic violation in Newtown. The White officer accused Lance of blowing a stop sign. Lance protested that was not the case and the officer cut him off and refused to allow him to speak. It was a classic ticket quota and there was no discussion allowed. If Lance had been White he would have had the chance to plead his side of the story rather than having been blocked with no chance to dispute the alleged violation.

Last, when Lance sought to find a gym close by to work out, he went to the Newtown Athletic Club (referred to as Newtown Aryan Club by folks of color and anti-racist Whites) to try out the gym. This was the club where Trump spoke during his campaign rally with full support of the owner, a prominent county Republican. Lance noticed right away the members of the club were all White but that didn't bother him. What shocked him was that he was given a tour but at no point did sales folks engage him in signing up or discussing a contract or options. Having lived in multiple locations worldwide and been a member of many gyms, he was stunned that he was given no additional information nor informed how to sign up for a membership. After these incidents and a constant upswing in local and national hate incidents and increasingly overt White supremacy, we attended a local Bucks County anti-hate rally with hundreds of other in late August of 2017. I made a double-sided sign challenging racism and we and our signs were covered in the local *Bucks Courier-Times* and on a brief interview with Philly Channel 6 news sharing that we were angry about racism—not sad:

http://6abc.com/solidarity-vigil-held-at-garden-of-reflection/2312487/ .

GUN CONTROL: MARCH FOR OUR LIVES AND ROAD TO CHANGE

I've been anti-war and anti-gun from as early as I can remember. In middle school, I remember Huth Upper Grades Center (Matteson, IL) history teacher Rita Kaonohi had us study African American poets including civil rights and anti-war activists Nikki Giovanni and Langston Hughes, a few years after the Vietnam War had ended. At age 18 I signed up for the draft as a conscientious objector because I wasn't about to fight rich men's wars for profit even as a teenager.

My first memory of gunfire was when I had bought a condo in Chicago's gentrifying Buena Park section of Uptown and nightly could hear it in alleys at a distance. Since we met in Chicago and lived in Uptown, Lance and I have been for nationwide gun control in the USA. But even with strong gun control ordinances in Illinois and Chicago, bordering Indiana was the problem as guns flowed over the border easily from a state with some of the most lax gun laws. My students at Lehman College in the Bronx, most of whom are women of color, have shared numerous stories of their fears and tracking of their Black and Brown sons, brothers, and fathers at the hands of mostly White NYPD officers over the years due to racist policing a lack of good training and accountability for police brutality. None have had children or teens killed, but all know plenty who have. It doesn't have to be this way.

Having watched constant police brutality with having followed #BlackLivesMatter on Twitter and Facebook, we've become more engaged in the need to end the school-to-prison pipeline, police brutality, and the military-industrial-prison complex: How wealthy White capitalists profit off of Black and Brown lives and injustice. The numbers of mass shootings using assault rifles has been outrageous with hundreds of children and young adults massacred from Sandy Hook, the Newtown, CT elementary school, to the outdoor concert in Las Vegas, NV, to the gay nightclub in Orlando, FL, to high school students and staff in Parkland, FL. We've donated annually to the Brady Campaign against gun violence and in 2018 to Change The Ref, the father of one of the slain Parkland students Manuel Oliver, an artist dedicating his career to the memory of his son Guac using public urban art to fight for gun control. We cheered the thousands of new teen activists from @AMarchForOurLives and @RoadtoChange to stop the National Rifle Association blood money and shift politicians to saving lives not guns.

Kalani's high school is across the street from our GOP congressperson's office and hundreds of high school students marched on his office in Spring of 2018 as part of the March for Our Lives movement. While Kalani was with other high school students at the rally, I was one of a small handful of parents with a poster I made stating "Arm Me with More School Counselors not Guns" challenging those who irrationally believe that more guns in schools prevent gun violence.

After the students were addressed by Congressperson Fitzpatrick's chief of staff, I stayed behind, introduced myself, and asked for a meeting as I'd never been able to get the Congressperson to meet with me for the over two years he'd been in office. He said we would arrange it but later emailed that the Congressperson couldn't see me but I could meet with the chief of staff instead. At that meeting I hoped to present my goals in seeing how bipartisan national legislation could be crafted to increase the numbers of school counselors and lower school counselor-to-student ratios nationwide (they are about 1:475 currently and 20% of students have no access to a school counselor) to reduce violence. The meeting never happened, which was not due to my multiple attempts.

I was the lead author on new regulations for school counselors and school counselor education master's programs that were voted into law in New York State in 2017 by the New York State Board of Regents, and with that victory we were able to require school counseling programs in all K-12 schools for the first time that must be developed and implemented by certified school counselors. A parent from Kalani's high school who works in the office reached out to me but reversed the chief of staff and said the congressperson would meet with me (I'm still waiting as of Spring 2019). In the meantime I worked with my state senate and state representative's offices on increasing school counselors in Pennsylvania as a gun violence reduction strategy, as well as a college access/affordability strategy.

When the Parkland shootings occurred on Valentine's Day we were horrified at the senseless loss of life. But Parkland, Florida was a wealthy suburb with many socially conscious students and parents who rallied to fight back without violence. Over the months, I followed on twitter teens who were leading the way and developed A March For Change and Road To Change linking intersectionality with urban students of color and suburban White students nationwide to take on the NRA and challenge bought-and-sold politicians who take NRA money that kills children, teens, and adults.

I also followed artist Manuel Oliver and his wife Patricia, whose son Guac was murdered that day as they now cross the country producing urban art installations to challenge the NRA and the politicians they finance who refuse to end gun violence. Change the Ref has become a powerful symbol of parents fighting back peacefully along with teens to end gun violence in the USA.

In the summer of 2018, teens from Parkland and elsewhere around the USA came to Perkasie, PA on a stop of the Road to Change tour to support the 225 high school students who were suspended by Pennridge School District officials for walking out and organizing against gun violence in Bucks County about 30 minutes north of where we live. Lance and I attended the talk and we were inspired by local and distant teens coming together across urban/suburban and diverse ethnic/racial, gender, and sexualities calling for an end to gun violence, better education, and the need to register to vote out politicians standing in the way of gun reform. During the public Question and Answer session, I asked the panel of students what they had learned from their trip, their organizing, and their fight to push for gun control. Multiple students answered that a whole new generation of activists had been awakened and it has influenced their potential majors in college and career trajectories.

CHALLENGING IMMIGRATIONISM & FAMILY DETENTION/SEPARATION

Part of why Lance and I identify as Green Party members, and as socialists, is that we have watched capitalist excesses, propelled by corporate Democrats' neoliberal agendas, and Republicans' neoconservative agendas, cause harm in the USA and around the world. Both parties are run by the interests of billionaires and corporations. We, however, agree with Greens, who put people, peace, and planet before profits. The latest horror in the USA has been continued attacks on immigrants and asylum seekers at the USA/Mexico border due to South and Central Americans (particularly Guatemalans and Hondurans) as well as Mexicans, fleeing violence and gangs that often resulted from USA policies attacking leftist governments, politicians, and citizens who challenge the excesses of capitalism including ongoing attempts at a coup in Venezuela to steal oil. Both USA corporate parties developed the Homeland Security department after 9/11 and one of its enforcement arms, ICE. The Obama administration deported more immigrants seeking a new life in the USA than any other USA administration. But the #45 administration took the policy and made it worse. Attorney General Sessions quoted *the Bible* to condone family separation. Massive rallies occurred across the USA at child/family detention sites (including one in Pennsylvania, Berks Detention Center) and in cities and towns, at ICE offices, and abroad from expatriates appalled at how illegallly the #USA government is treating children and families and criminalizing those fleeing violence often been caused by USA capitalist policies in Latin America.

In response I have challenged my state representatives via @Twitter, letters, phone calls, and visits to their offices. Lance and I attended a protest of over 250 people at GOP congressperson Brian Fitzpatrick's office and went inside to meet with his Chief of Staff, who didn't want to engage in a frank discussion claiming it was almost Father's Day weekend. Oh, the irony with hundreds of fathers being forcibly separated from their kids as part of USA immigration policy.

I carried a sign reading "Families Belong Together" and we added it to a huge wall of children's toys, book, and posters condemning the separation of children from their families and family detention. But with droves of voters flooding the office, it showed that protests and speaking up work. The following week, congressperson Fitzpatrick came out against family separation and agreed to work toward ending it with a visit to one of the detention centers in Texas (but not Berks Detention Center in Pennsylvania!). Words were not enough: He has not sponsored and legislative or investigative action into the abuse of children and clear human rights and international law violations.

Soon afterward, the White House, after voluminous protests, reversed course and said it would end family separation but not attempt to reunite families already separated (estimated to be over 3,000). Months later, hundreds of families have yet to be reunited past a judge's order requiring the government to act. Many more families, it turns out, were separated with no records kept than were originally reported in the media. We are thankful as long time American Civil Liberties Union ACLU members for the many attorneys and judges who continue to fight the illegal, immoral, unconstitutional, and unethical anti-immigrant policies being perpetrated by ICE and the GOP-backed #45 administration.

Two weeks later, Lance and I attended the local Doylestown, PA rally to end family separation/detention developed by RiseUp Doylestown and co-sponsored by the Bucks County Green Party and other local organizations. I carried a "SHUT DOWN BERKS" sign and we protested with hundreds of others to reunite families and stop deportations. The USA struggle for equity and challenging multiple oppressions continued as struggles for marriage equality and LGBTQ rights were equally on our minds (and in person) in Taiwan.

CHAPTER TWENTY-TWO

TAIWAN GAY MARRIAGE STRUGGLE

In March of 2017, we took advantage of Kalani's two-week spring break and returned to Taiwan for a vacation and activism. We did two presentations: One on sexuality education and our family story for 150 graduate counseling students at National Changhua University of Education (NCUE) and one streamed live on Facebook as a benefit for the Taiwan LGBT Family Rights Advocacy Association at a lesbian-owned cafe in Taipei. We had great feedback from both presentations and we were amazed at the growth in numbers of LGBTQ-headed families in Taiwan and those who seek to become parents. At NCUE, in a room of 150 students, we were the first gay parents and teen that any of the students had encountered. After 20+ years of presenting on LGBTQ and couple and family issues, there are always fascinating new questions from audiences. But after many trips to Taiwan where Lance had to do more work than play, this trip was primarily for fun.

The summer prior to the 2016 USA presidential election, we saw a second documentary in New York City done by Taiwanese-American filmmaker and CUNY professor Larry Tung on transgender activist Dr. Pauline Park's return to Korea as a trans-racial adoptee. We had not seen either of them in years and Larry asked if anyone had done a documentary about our family prior to the screening. We said we had been in various videos and news clips but no traditional documentary. He was interested featuring our story for submission to LGBTQ and other film festivals internationally. A month later he offered to produce a documentary on our story as a dual-national two-generation queer family. We didn't know, until that time, that Larry was born and raised in Taichung, and that is where his parents reside. During this trip in Taiwan, Larry started filming us and Lance's sisters. The documentary, tentatively entitled, "My Rainbow Family," was scheduled for release in 2019.

THE ALISHAN MOUNTAIN RAILWAY CAR

Our first leg of the trip was flying to Taiwan's Kinmen Island, as none of us had been there as it is close to China and west of the main island of Taiwan. We toured with brother #6, Chun, a professor of urban planning specializing in architectural preservation, who took us through all 12 original Chinese family villages, including the Chen family village. This was the closest we have been to Lance's parents' hometown, which was about 30 miles northwest of Kinmen Island in China's Fujian province. Next, we returned to the Taiwan mainland for another first--the annual Cherry Blossom festival on Alishan mountain. At the peak of the mountain, we rode in one of three mountaintop railway systems left in the world, and when we boarded the train, Lance was asked by a woman about where Kalani's "mom" was. Even though this was vacation, teachable moments were always around the corner. Lance debated about whether he wanted to tell the story or not in a train car full of strangers listening intently. He decided to share the story and they learned how Kalani came into the world and that Kalani had two gay dads. This was an especially heart warming experience as we received praise for being gay dads from all the train car riders. It evidenced that even in rural Taiwan, there has been a dramatic positive change in attitudes toward affirming LGBTQ persons and families, particularly parents with children (despite conservative referenda). The research indicates direct personal experiences with LGBTQ persons is key to ending heterosexism and genderism over time.

THE TAXI DRIVER

Next, we wanted to see the new southern branch of the Taiwan National Museum pan-Asian cultural exhibits and the new building's stunning modern design and grounds. Another teachable moment arose in the taxi ride on the way to the museum from the High Speed Rail station. The driver inquired if Lance was touring his "American friends" around. Lance shared our story of being more than "friends." After hearing our story, the taxi driver said he finally understood why he should support gay marriage. He was excited to have "famous" customers and insisted on stopping and taking a picture of us at the end of the ride. We found more LGBTQ-parenting affirmation from another rural Taiwanese who supported marriage equality with the experience of meeting first-hand a two-dad family with a teenager.

MEETUP WITH NEW GAY DADS AND THEIR BABIES

Back in Taipei we attended a luncheon with members of the Taiwan gay dads' group. We were inspired to see so many babies age 2 and under. Kalani, at 13.5, was quite the guh-guh (older "brother") to a mini-gayby boom across Taiwan. It was humbling to hear stories from how folks saw our pictures and heard our story over the past 20+ years either from public lectures or media coverage, and that gave them hope and inspiration that one day, they could be dads via surrogacy or adoption (and sometimes the traditional way via heterosexual marriages left at the wayside). But for most gay men in Taiwan, cost is prohibitive and surrogacy remains illegal and takes much time, money and effort outside of Taiwan. Adoptions are limited in Taiwan as well, so creating LGBTQ-parented families remains a challenge financially and culturally for LGBTQ persons in a nation with great economic disparity between the wealthy and everyone else, although not as wide a disparity as in the United States and with Taiwan's better social supports.

MEETUP WITH LESBIAN MOMS AND THEIR KIDS

We also traveled to Taichung and stayed with Lance's mom for several days and spent time with extended family and friends. As backstory, about a decade ago, Lance was in touch with Taichung resident Chen Su and her partner (now wife, thanks to Canadian gay marriage laws) about the possibility of our assisting them to create a family. At that time, we met for vegetarian lunch in downtown Taichung and when they asked us if we would be sperm donors, we were floored. We were flattered but felt put on the spot. We knew that the legal entanglements, without knowing them well, were not something we wanted to risk at that time. A decade later, via Facebook, Lance had stayed in touch with them applauding their successful surrogacy with twins via a White Canadian sperm donor, and we had the chance to meet their elementary-age kids on this trip. Their children were bright, outgoing, energetic, and playful and we were excited to see that they had taken the plunge to go public and come out as lesbian moms with children via international surrogacy in a national Taiwan magazine article. Chen had been outed by a colleague but in the end it turned out well. Then, just after the Taiwan Supreme Court announced marriage equality would be the law of the land in two years if the Executive Yuan didn't act earlier, Chen was quoted in the *New York Times*. Like many others in Taiwan and the Taiwanese/Asian LGBTQ diaspora, she credited knowing us and our story was central to their journey and dreams of becoming lesbian moms even if we provided a slight detour for them along the way. After our visit, we left to prepare for a large lecture and discussion at National Changhua University of Education.

SEXUALITY EDUCATION, LGBTQ FAMILIES, AND KALANI'S IDENTITIES

We cherish our bond with Dr. Sharon Shu-chu Chao, our constant ally for LGBTQ rights, since we first met in 2006. Every time we are in Taiwan, we do a lecture at NCUE for graduate students in counseling, undergraduates, alumni, and the public on our story, surrogacy, LGBTQ couples, sexuality education, and raising Kalani, who now identifies as a queer, pansexual, non-binary teen and uses the pronouns they and them. What made this lecture and presentation unique was the sophistication of the questions about LGBTQ issues and sexuality education. It showed, too, Taiwan's adoption of comprehensive gender and sexuality education K-12 has had a positive effect on the consciousness of all students in the country. It is no wonder that conservative Christians, financed by USA billionaires, were rallying to end LGBTQ education in K-8 schools via public referendum in late 2018 (although the government refused to make any changes). Our presence was an antidote to the far-right reactionary forces seeking a return to ignorance related to LGBTQ families and sexuality.

MEDIA APPEARANCES

Journalists continued to give voice to our story in Taiwan and the USA. Andrew Ryan, co-host of Taiwan Public Television's *"From Hear to There,"* interviewed us in 2016 with his co-host at Grounds for Sculpture, The Little Chef bakery, and Princeton University as part of their Season 3 Episode 6, which aired in the Spring of 2017. We did a little singing in the rain as the interview proceeded:

http://pics.ee/v-1402395 (our segment starts at 33:00).

The show, a travelogue that features the sights and sounds of Taiwan and travels abroad featuring the playful commentary of host Andrew Ryan, who grew up gay in the USA, speaks Mandarin and English, and has lived in Taiwan for 20 years, and co-host Hsin-Ting Lin, a Taiwan native who is a straight marathon runner, dancer, and blind. The travelogue focuses on sounds and sights for inclusive travel. The most interesting part was watching co-host Hsin-Ting touch one of the sculptures and do a spontaneous interactive dance interpreting the piece of art with his body.

In Taiwan, we were interviewed by gay dad Jay Lin's LGBTQ media company, GaGaTai.com/LaLaTai.com, on LGBTQ parenting, sexuality education, and marriage equality. The video clip featured us jet-lagged after our NYC flight into Taipei and Kalani was eloquent talking about a variety of their experiences in elementary, middle, and high school on sexuality and gender issues:

https://www.youtube.com/watch?v=rG5X_eXJTvQ . The clip has become one of the most viewed LGBTQ clips in Taiwan with 95,000 hits on YouTube.

Soon after this video aired, I saw a #MyAsianAmericanFamily hashtag trending on Twitter and tweeted out a picture of our family and it landed in a *Huffington Post* article:

http://www.huffingtonpost.com/entry/my-asian-american-family_us_5919fd75e4b05dd15f0a427d

Back in the United States, Taiwan's *Mirror Media* sent a reporter and film crew to spend the weekend with us in Newtown, PA for an in-depth article and video with numerous family photographs. Lance's coming out story as the first out Taiwanese gay dad was the focus: Coming out to traditional Taiwanese parents, how we met as a couple, the journey toward parenting, the legal roadblocks, and Kalani's perspective as a queer non-binary teen with gay dads. The story had numerous links:

https://www.mirrormedia.mg/story/20170712pol004/

https://www.mirrormedia.mg/story/20170712pol005/

https://www.mirrormedia.mg/story/20170712pol006/

https://www.mirrormedia.mg/story/20170712pol007/

https://www.mirrormedia.mg/story/20170712pol002/

https://www.mirrormedia.mg/story/20170712pol003/

No summer was complete without some good beach, international travel, and activism reading. *Gay Parent Magazine* included an article when I was interviewed in 2015 about our travels to Taiwan, why it is a great place for LGBTQ travel, favorite destinations, and activism for LGBTQ families and marriage equality. The article celebrated the May 2017 Taiwan Supreme Court ruling on making gay marriage the law of the land within two years if the legislature didn't act sooner.

TAIWAN SUPREME COURT MARRIAGE EQUALITY RULING

We were in the USA when the Taiwan Supreme Court ruled for marriage equality in the Spring of 2017. I was driving Kalani to high school when I heard the news and I had tears in my eyes. It was shocking to hear that the work of so many Taiwanese LGBTQ activists and allies had come to this moment--the first Asian nation appeared to be on the verge of marriage equality. Did our video admonition to Tsai-Ing Wen pay off? She didn't act though--after her DPP party chased LGBTQ votes with a promise of marriage equality she and her party backed away from supporting it after she was elected president of Taiwan. But the Taiwan Supreme Court ruled in favor of LGBTQ marriage. As a family, we will continue to share our story in Taiwan and the greater Taiwanese/Chinese diaspora and in the USA about supporting LGBTQ parenting, comprehensive sexuality education, dual-national citizenship, surrogacy, and LGBTQ equality.

With the Taiwan Supreme Court ruling, we decided it was time to test the future law and secure Taiwan citizenship for Kalani as a dual national with the first attempt of two men having their names on both an international birth certificate and an international marriage license. In July of 2017, Lance sent the paperwork to Atlanta to have the Taiwan Economic and Cultural Office (TECO) verify Kalani's birth certificate. In August, Lance, Kalani, and I went to the TECO office on 42nd street in Manhattan to have Kalani's Taiwan passport created and make official their dual-national citizenship.

For me, it will take longer before I can be a dual national; I don't want to give up my USA citizenship and currently Taiwan would grant me permanent resident status as I only speak conversational Mandarin (ironic that in the USA I have White privilege, English language, and immigration privilege, but in Taiwan, I am the potential target of homophobia, linguicism, and immigrationism). In early 2018, Taiwan announced a list of countries where Taiwanese spouses of LGBTQ residents who could be permanent residents and the USA was included. I'm happy I'm on the list but I don't think Taiwan should make a list of approved in an oppressive hierarchy of who gets residence status. When Taiwan allows me full dual citizenship through gay marriage, I'm ready.

Unfortunately, trying to procure Kalani's dual-national citizenship proved institutional heterosexism lurked in Taiwan's immigration office. After learning that we would have to wait for an email from Taiwan directly (instead of completing the passport process and finalizing their citizenship at the TECO office in NYC), Lance received an email stating he had to appear in person in Taiwan to prove he was Kalani's father since they were born "out of wedlock." The English terminology was so hateful; Kalani was born out of love and a committed legal relationship of two gay dads. An added insult was when the staffer said that Kalani's Chinese name, which has four characters instead of the traditional three, didn't meet traditional language standards. Lance posted what happened on Facebook and immediately received an offer of help from a gay attorney in Taiwan specializing in LGBTQ issues and immigration law and and additional support from one of the leaders of the Taiwan LGBT Family Rights Advocacy Association.

Lance wrote that he had sent a valid birth certificate for Kalani and that our marriage license was over six years old in the USA and Lance would have been thrilled to apply for Kalani's dual national citizenship at birth but gay marriage was illegal in the USA and Taiwan when Kalani was born and Lance refused to deny being gay to get dual citizenship for Kalani. After much back and forth, the NYC TECO office booted the issue to the Taipei office and then the Taipei office booted it back to NYC.

While we developed infinite patience as gay dads, for every barrier that stood in our way, we found a way to go over, under, or around. Unlike heterosexual parents, Lance had to find multiple legal records for the Taiwan officials including my legal adoption of Kalani in 2004. Fortunately, our attorney, Bill Singer, had a copy of it in his records ready to send abroad. It seemed that the TECO Office was stonewalling us because Kalani was conceived through surrogacy, which is illegal in Taiwan.

But since we were in the USA for Kalani's entire conception to birth process and again for my legal adoption, this was an unfair barrier as other Taiwanese of varied sexual orientations have gone outside Taiwan in pursuit of surrogacy and had their children recognized as Taiwan citizens by applying as "single" parents or with a birth certificate including the name of the birth mother/surrogate. Fortunately, the lawyer in the NYC TECO office was assigned to work with Lance was supportive.

In August of 2018, Lance received word from the TECO office in New York City that the passport application for Kalani (and citizenship) would be approved once Lance sent the certified copies of the paternity affidavit and court order to the Atlanta TECO office, which has jurisdiction over persons born in North Carolina, for document authentication. This meant, after 15 years, Kalani would soon officially be a dual national of Taiwan and the USA just like baba Lance. Lance posted the news to Facebook and many LGBTQ families in Taiwan and in the Taiwanese diaspora expressed great joy and excitement as Taiwan's first out gay dad was on the verge of making history again as part of the first gay married couple to get citizenship for their child (now a teenager) with two fathers' names on the birth certificate and on a wedding certificate.

But that good news brought more drama as the Atlanta TECO office said we didn't have the correct stamps on the birth certificates from Asheville, NC. So, Lance contacted the lesbian attorney in Asheville who assisted with the original birth certificate to get the correct stamps and send them to Atlanta on our behalf.

However, despite our personal family progress in overcoming heterosexism in Taiwan, there was troubling news in 2018 endangering the future of gay marriage in Taiwan. The Taiwan constitution was amended to allow for citizen referendums at a much lower level of voter signatures than in prior years. This was an ominous sign for LGBTQ marriage as social conservatives backed by evangelical Christians with billionaire money from wealthy conservative Christians in the USA created a referendum to stop gay marriage and K-8 LGBTQ sexuality and gender education.

To fight back, Taiwan LGBTQ activists created two new referenda: (1) to allow gay marriage, and (2) to continue to include LGBT sexuality and gender education in elementary and middle schools. Supporters needed to gather signatures to get on the ballot, but they started later than supporters of the anti-LGBT referenda. However, they collected over 550,000 signatures for gay marriage and 450,000 for sexuality education in 37 days to have the pro-gay marriage and sexuality education referenda on the November ballot alongside the anti-gay marriage and anti-sex education referenda. The support that the LGBTQ community gathered in such a short time was unprecedented in Taiwan's history.

Lance spent the month of October in Taiwan doing public speaking and media appearances and connecting with other Taiwan LGBTQ activists and staff from USA-based Marriage Equality. As Taiwan's first openly gay father, Lance wanted to be on the ground assisting in the fight for both the pro-gay marriage and pro-sexuality education referenda votes. He shared the story of how our family has been strengthened legally with gay marriage over the years for numerous audiences in person and in the media. Lance's speaking schedule included:

- Oct. 3, National Changhua University of Education, "Why Marriage Equality is Important" to over 100 undergraduates, master's and doctoral graduate students, and faculty in education;
- Oct. 5, KOO Foundation/Sun Yat-Sen Cancer Center, Taipei, "Why Marriage Equality is Important";
- Oct. 8, FTV (Formosa TV), Taipei, Taiwan Lecture Hall webcast program interview: "Human Rights: To Love and To Be Loved" on marriage equality;
- Oct. 16, Chungshan Medical University, Taichung, Graduate students and faculty in Public Health, "Why Marriage Equality is Important";
- Oct. 16, Ming Dao High School, Taichung, (Lance's alma mater), School Counseling and Dean of Students' staff, "Why Marriage Equality is Important";
- Oct. 20, National Taiwan University, Taipei, Physical Therapy Department, "Understanding Physical Therapists' Social Responsibilities from a Social Justice Perspective'" and on
- Oct. 24, Tofu Books, Chiayi, "LGBT Families and Marriage Equality."

His speaking on the FTV television program, one of Taiwan's commercial networks--was the first time one had featured any LGBTQ content in an interview format. Lance spoke in all of his presentations about our family and the importance of comprehensive sexuality eduation K-12 including LGBTQ issues and the need for marriage equality to protect couples and their children and to strengthen couples and families' success and mental health outcomes.

Lance attended Taiwan Pride, which almost doubled the prior record attendance with 140,000 persons in Taipei celebrating the theme--the need to vote for marriage equality and K-8 comprehensive sexuality education. Lance spoke to the crowds as he rode the float about the importance of pro-LGBTQ voting, assisted lesbian moms' kids to join in the parade along the way, and walked 20,000 steps of all four parade route areas handing out flyers about the importance of 2 yes votes for marriage equality and comprehensive sexuality referenda and 3 no votes on the right-wing anti-LGBTQ and anti-sexuality education referenda.

The time in Taiwan was energizing and exhausting as Lance was angered and saddened that the nation of his birth had been invaded by right-wing Christian conservatives and their USA-based millions trying to proselytize with money and buy the votes of Taiwanese conservatives based on hate and fear. Aligned with the conservative KMT party and fueled by mainland Chinese conservatives bent on wrestling Taiwan's independence away, LGBTQ individuals and families had become an ugly wedge issue in national elections and the future of an independent democracy.

Upon return to the United States on November 2, Lance was asked to speak at a fundraiser for Taiwan marriage equality held at New York City's Stonewall Inn, the national historic site honoring the key place of resistance in the modern gay rights movement where bar patrons bashed back after a police raid in 1969. Lance spoke the following words to the audience:

"Love from Stonewall Remarks: In favor of urgent funding to fight the right and support Taiwan's LGBTQ Marriage Equality referenda

Dear folks,

It's an honor to be invited to speak tonight. My name is Lance Chen-Hayes. I'm a cisgender gay man. I was born and raised in Taiwan. I'm a 24-year relationship with my husband, and we have a 15 year-old teen. I came out to my family 22 years ago when we planned our sacred commitment ceremony, i.e., the illegal wedding. At that time, we wanted to build a life together with our families and friends present regardless of what the law said. **All families deserve full legal protection.** Marriage equality is a fight that is dear to my heart. I've watched carefully since the marriage equality fight started in Taiwan many years ago. I'm also the first out gay dad in Taiwan to tell our gay family story to the public through many different media. When the Supreme Court in Taiwan ruled in favor of marriage equality within two years in 2017, we were elated. However, the anti-LGBTQ groups seized upon the opportunity to push for referenda to prevent same-gender couples from gaining full legal protection of marriage and to remove K-8 LGBTQ curriculum from Taiwan's Gender Equity Education law. Gender Equity Education has been in Taiwan's educational system since 2004, added K-12 LGBT curriculum in 2011, and has built a new generation of young people who are more open-minded and affirming of LGBTQ folks. Having this curriculum makes Taiwan a world leader in providing comprehensive sexuality education to all K-12 students and helps decrease bullying of LGBTQ students. Now the anti-LGBTQ groups want to take that away along with the chance for marriage equality.

I returned 3 days ago after spending a month in Taiwan doing presentations and interviews about my family's story and the need for marriage equality and comprehensive sexuality education K-12 that is LGBTQ-inclusive. I also saw how conservative USA-based Christian billionaires are funding the fight for marriage equality in Taiwan. Taiwan LGBT groups are out-spent by the anti-LGBT groups. They have a budget north of 1 billion NT (New Taiwan) dollars. That's over $33 million US dollars to spread fear, hate, and misinformation in a country the size of New Jersey. When I was in Taiwan, I saw evidence of their massive campaign everywhere in the north, central, south, and eastern parts of the country. I've seen banners hanging from storefronts and buildings. They hire people to give out flyers on the streets in multiple cities and rural areas. They buy TV and print newspaper ads and continue to blast inaccurate and hateful messages to the public. What worries me the most is how these negative messages have impacted and will continue to harm LGBT folks, especially young people. I've seen LGBT people angered, hurt, and losing hope from the constant barrage of hateful messages in public, in the media, and online. **To counteract the hate, it's important for us to show the love and financial support.**

When I'm in Taiwan, I always come out to strangers whenever possible and encourage other LGBTs to do the same. For example, one time a taxi driver asked if I was touring my "American friends" around. I immediately told him that "this is my HUSBAND and this is OUR teen," and proceeded to share more stories about our family. By the time we got to the hotel, the taxi driver told me that now he understood the importance of gay marriage and he would support it. I'm telling this story because we can change regular folks' minds if we educate them with stories of love and equity, and give them accurate information. That's why we need to financially support what marriage equality folks in Taiwan are doing: Working around the clock with a small budget to produce materials and information to educate people to show people stories of

LGBT love and the need for marriage equality and K-12 sex education equity. If you can read Chinese, you can access the www.equallove.tw website, and on the upper tabs there is a set of tools to help counter misinformation. Or, if you have Line (the Taiwanese group chat app), you can do an ID search using @2yes3no to access the information, or follow on twitter @equallovetw. Marriage equality folks in Taiwan need our financial support so they can reach more people and change more people's minds and get out the November referenda vote. They need more money to buy time slots for TV ads with positive LGBTQ marriage equality and sex education messages. **We are in the final stretch right now in the last three weeks prior to the vote and we cannot let hate speech dominate in public, on social media, or in print advertising or on cable/TV stations."**

Lance and I and many other activists agree civil society should not be voting on civil and human rights. The results of the referenda, however, were deeply disappointing. Voters in rural areas of Taiwan were manipulated by disinformation and hate organized by the conservative Christians who successfully passed the anti-gay marriage Prop. 8 in California. A small group of wealthy conservatives in Taiwan used similar tactics and funding from wealthy USA-based evangelical Christians.

Horrifically, multiple LGBT folks in Taiwan committed suicide in the aftermath of the no vote due to family rejection. It's appalling what hate did in Taiwan. But, the antidote is grieving our losses and finding stronger ways to fight the hate with education and backing political candidates who are pro-LGBTQ in action, not only in words. As heartbroken and angered as we were at the results of the referenda, which meant the marriage equality and K-8 LGBTQ sexuality education votes went down to defeat, it only emboldened us and our activist colleagues to fight harder.

When the Taiwan national government offices stated the referenda were nonbinding and that gay marriage would go forward and that K-8 education would continue to include LGBTQ curricula, we felt relieved and vindicated. We are wary, however, as we hope that in May of 2019 the legislation to be voted on will be full marriage equality—be it a separate law or amending the Taiwan Constitution. The bill introduced in March of 2019 was close to marriage equality but lacked rights for all international partners to become citizens and did not provide for adoption using IVF or surrogacy. Nonetheless, on December 7th, 2018, Kalani's Taiwan passport arrived in the mail making them the first dual national USA Taiwan citizen with 2 dads' names on both an international birth certificate and an international marriage license.

AFTERWORD

The fight for LGBTQ rights and social justice continues…..

NQAPIA CONFERENCE

In July of 2018 Lance attended the tri-annual National Queer Asian Pacific Islander Alliance (NQAPIA) conference in San Francisco, and we presented as a family on our activism for LGBTQ rights in Taiwan and the USA. As donors to NQAPIA, we supported their unique mission in person as the issues of oppression facing queer APIs are urgent in the USA with increased classist, homophobic, immigrationist, racist, sexist, and transphobic incidents and challenges on civil and human rights policies by the #45 administration, the Republican Party, and conservative billionaires and the media outlets they finance. We had not traveled to the Bay Area in over a decade, and the trip provided a chance to reconnect with Lance's Taiwan high school friends, other Taiwanese gay dads, my college roommate, my former partner, and a former student of mine from Chicago who has been active in HIV/AIDS counseling and advocacy since the mid-1990s. Lance found the conference electrifying and a new activism focus for retirement. He has focused LGBTQ activism on immigration rights, Asian and Pacific Islander parents and friends of LGBTQ children and teens, and LGBTQ aging issues using his skills as a dual-national Taiwanese gay dad trained as a physical therapist.

KALANI REUNITED AND HANGING WITH THE GAY LIBERATION FRONT

After NQAPIA, we were contacted by Richard Koob, co-founder of the Kalani Honua Eco-resort, who asked if we would like to spend a long weekend with him, his sister, her wife, and daughter in Manhattan and then travel with him to meet with two of his Gay Liberation Front (GLF) colleagues in the Bronx and Massachusetts and travel to gay retreat venues in Vermont. Richard, a dancer, LGBT rights and HIV/AIDS activist for decades, was an original GLF member in New York City in 1970. Our Kalani had the chance to meet Richard in person for the first night of this trip as the last time they'd seen each other, Kalani was a year old in Hawai'i. Kalani returned home to Pennsylvania and we continued on a brief New England journey with Richard. He introduced us to Bronx-based Perry Brass, a GLF member and writer on gay issues since the early 70s. Then we drove to Massachusetts to meet Allen Young, another prolific GLF member who released a memoir about his life as a gay and environmental activist. We read the memoir in Allen's rural Massachusetts home while staying with him and then drove to Vermont's Radical Faerie Camp Destiny, where Allen and

Richard spoke about their work with GLF and beyond as gay activists and early founders of the movement, and we shared our work in Taiwan and the USA as the next generation and as gay dads. We ended the trip with a visit to Frog Meadow, the queer men's retreat inspired by the owners' visit to Kalani eco-resort in the early 2000s. If not for Richard, Allen, Perry, and the rest of the original GLF members' agitating and organizing in the streets of NYC, we would not be together as a couple, let alone have created a family. With the Stonewall Riots' 50th anniversary in 2019, it was an honor to travel with three of the men who helped start the modern gay civil rights movement and share how our journeys have been linked as we create the next queer generations thanks to their spirits, sensuality, organizing, and writing.

A CELEBRATION OF PAST AND FUTURE ACCOMPLISHMENTS

In summer of 2018, we celebrated two milestones in our life. I was promoted to full professor at Lehman College. Lance, after neck surgery in the Spring to remove two herniated discs, celebrated the end of his recovery and 31 years of pediatric and geriatric physical therapy by retiring from work as a physical therapist. We celebrated on my birthday with friends, family, and colleagues at our home with dinner and cake from Princeton, New Jersey's Little Chef and WildFlour bakeries. Lance was excited to have a long rest and time for taking art classes and focusing on activism.

ANTI-FASCIST RALLY

In January of 2019 a White Supremacist group threatened to march in Princeton, NJ. Having joined Democratic Socialists of America a week prior, it was our chance to go and rally on behalf of the counter-demonstration organizers, Central New Jersey Democratic Socialists. Hundreds of Princeton area high school students, Princeton University students, socialists, Greens, and Democrats marched against hate. There were lots of Black Lives Matter posters, and plenty of rainbow flags, many creative chalkings on the sidewalk, and constant chants against #45, KKK, fascists, and the GOP. Lance and I, as a mixed-race gay couple, were thrilled when we learned that the socialist-led rally frightened away the White Supremacists from marching. The rally, instead, became a demonstration of love and anti-oppression forces over hate, fear, fascism, and multiple oppressions. We have to be in the streets to counter hate, fascism, and oppressions.

#REDFORED and @CUNYSTRUGGLE

Then in February, NYC activists kicked out Amazon and the $3B gift from two centrist Democrats who learned their lesson on not involving the public in decision-making. That money should be spent on adequately funding K-12 city schools, ending homelessness, fixing the subways, and paying a living wage to CUNY adjunct faculty who teach a majority of classes on our 22 campuses but don't make a living wage while doing it. As a union activist, I had closely followed the last few years of the #RedForEd movement in K-12 public schools and supported their efforts wholeheartedly in Red states and increasingly in large cities with more progressive voters. In CUNY, I felt the union leadership, like so many K-12 teachers and their unions, was not responsive to members who see strikes as the only tool to get politicians to adequately fund schools to support student learning and educators at the same time. To assist this process, I joined with the CUNY activist group, CUNYSTRUGGLE, and shared the story of how I brought forward a $7KorStrike resolution at Lehman College in our PSC-CUNY chapter meeting that was passed successfully the prior December. It emboldened me to continue organizing with @CUNYSTRUGGLE and as of February my campus is holding weekly #RedForEd actions as more and more union members come to the conclusion that striking is the only way we will get our demands met:

7K or Strike Resolution Passes at Lehman Despite Some Drama

By Stuart Chen-Hayes

As a full professor at CUNY's Lehman College, I've been a member of the PSC-CUNY since being hired as an assistant professor on the tenure track. I believe in the power of activist unions and know that the real power is always with the rank-and-file, or should be, if we take the reins. My dad was a high school teacher in suburban Chicago and I remember walking picket lines with him, and how he was mistreated by administration for being a union activist. So I'm a second-generation unionist.

For years I was more focused on citywide PSC actions and organizing and didn't participate much in the Lehman chapter. But a couple of years ago a new chapter chair was elected and I sensed a change in style and leadership and wanted to be more involved. I went to two citywide CUNY rallies this year. The first was a show of solidarity and the speaker was Governor Cuomo. I was truly disappointed because I know just how detrimental his policies have been toward workers, unions, and especially K-16 public education. When he spoke, I chose to hang out with other socialists at the socialist table – that was empowering. The second rally I attended with this fall in front of Bill Thompson's office. That's where I met up with the CUNY Struggle folks. I'd met a number of the organizers at the Left Forum this summer as well so folks recognized me. I asked for literature and said I wouldn't have a graduate program without my part-timers, who deserve $7K – and what we've been doing in PSC has not been enough. So I got involved for the first time outside the PSC and New Caucus structures.

At our mid-semester Lehman Chapter meeting I passed out flyers from CUNY Struggle on the 7K or Strike movement. I then worked with the current chapter chair to see if we could get a vote on the resolution. Earlier in the semester he'd asked me to write up a paragraph about #RedForEd to share with the chapter. But he never sent it. I asked why and he said that there was a problem because I had included a sentence mentioning the campaign for 7K or Strike. I said that we had academic freedom why would he not send that out? He said he personally agreed with 7K or Strike, so that was great, at least.

I then pushed for a resolution on 7K or Strike at Lehman. After considerable back and forth we got an agreement to discuss the resolution at our chapter meeting on December 5th. I sent the original CUNY Struggle resolution from the Graduate Center, titled "7K or Strike." When the agenda went, however, it only said "$7K" resolution…"or Strike" was missing. *Hmmm…* was that a typo or was there mischief afoot? You guessed it! Academics don't make THAT kind of typo by accident.

I had 40 copies of the resolution for the meeting and handed them out along with the flyer. I had also handed out copies at a meeting about a month earlier so that people could think about it, though we had not discussed it then. The chapter vice-chair led the meeting as the chair was at a conference out of town. The first half of the meeting was taken up by a PSC organizer who spoke on various issues about membership, and the vice-chair, who gave updates on the ongoing contract campaign. We got to the resolution at 4:20, with only 40 minutes to go (and I had to teach back-to-back classes starting at 5!). The vice-chair began by claiming any resolution that wasn't approved by PSC central leadership would need a quorum of over 78 persons in the room to approve it.

That was news to me. I asked if there had ever in the history of the chapter been 78 folks at any meeting. The vice-chair said that he did not believe so. The vice-chair then asked me to introduce the resolution. I stood and argued that I wouldn't have a graduate program without part-timers, and that the cost of living in NYC is impossible for those who are living on

$3K per course. I said that we must fight public officials just gave away $3B of our tax dollars without public input to the world's richest man, Jeff Bezos, when all of that money could instead be paying for 7K for adjuncts and free college! I asked how many folks knew about #RedForEd, and how in right-to-work red states across the country this year we've seen K-12 teachers shut their schools down statewide to fight for decent wages and fair working conditions to support their students. Moreover, I added, many of these folks did so as Trump voters, and in states where union leaders ignored them, disagreed with them, or hadn't organized effectively in years. I also shared that for the first time ever this week Charter School teachers in Chicago are out on strike, having organized with Chicago Teachers Union Local 1, which was also the inspiration for other #RedForEd strikes nationwide.

Members in attendance discussed the issue of striking, job actions, and solidarity, all clearly in sympathy with my general points. Some however were hesitant to do anything that would trigger the Taylor Law. Then, unexpectedly, an executive committee member and the vice-chair shared a different resolution that did not challenge the PSC leadership, and did not call for a strike, though it mentioned potentially building toward actions that could include a strike. Robert's Rules were quickly invoked to ensure that that particular resolution was voted on first. In discussion, I asked who wrote the second resolution and was told that the current chapter chair had written it two nights before, based on the resolution that passed at BMCC! Well, it went up for a vote first, and it failed.

After this brief interlude we were back to my resolution, written by CUNY Struggle. Several amendments were discussed and voted upon, which preserved the spirit of the resolution and added more specifics about building toward a strike. At 4:59, the amended resolution was approved and passed by a majority of members in the room. The next day, a version of the resolution was sent by the chapter vice chair, with several added paragraphs from the BMCC version, to certain chapter members and the PSC organizer. Gone was the final paragraph stating the pledge to authorize a strike. That wasn't what we voted on. I am presently working to get this corrected, and hope to have a finalized version of the resolution we voted on as soon as possible.

It certainly looks like there's a game plan passed down from on high to defang this resolution, where they start with #1 and then move down to #6 as each domino falls:

1. Try to avoid ever having this discussion or ever letting it on the agenda.
2. Waste time in the meeting before the resolution comes up.

3. Focus on procedural issues, emphasizing a lack of official quorum (which our meetings never have).
4. Talk about the Taylor law in hopes that people will vote no.
5. Argue that strike is the last thing you do and it is therefore too early to discuss it; this line of thinking could lead to tabling the resolution or sending it out to committee.
6. Introduce a substitute resolution approved by central leadership.

In the end, the resolution passed. But the lesson learned here? PSC-CUNY needs to become a democratic union. It is simply not that right now. There is no way that one-party rule, currently the New Caucus, represents the rank-and-file. With Janus at hand, we need to build membership and take actions that fight to increase democracy. This type of anti-rank-and-file behavior is not the way to do it.

I'm thrilled to have had my first union resolution passed and look forward to more. I invite others, especially other full-timers, to join in the fight for 7K and for a democratic union. I know I've had many Lehman folks reach out as part of this event and that we will be organizing further despite folks attempting to block our attempts. Thanks also to Dr. Lois Weiner who invited me to be part of the international @teachsolidarity collective online, and to her wonderful writing about teacher unionism. I will be teaching her book on the subject this spring in my Leadership and Advocacy in Schools class. Last, I am inspired by many educators, unionists, and privatization foes on Twitter. It's where I have learned much about organizing for justice. Solidarity!

Since December, multiple other teacher unions have gone on strike and successfully settled contract demands including Los Angeles teachers, Denver teachers, a second charter strike in Chicago (the nations' 3rd charter strike), and teachers walked out again in West Virginia and were scheduled to do so in Oakland, CA with Sacramento not far behind. At the university level, Wright State teachers ended their strike successfully, and more CUNY faculty were coming to the conclusion that we need to be on strike as well.

REFLECTIONS ON 25 YEARS OF LOVE AND STRUGGLE

When I look back on the last two-and-a-half decades for us as a couple and the last decade-and-a-half as parents, it's been fast, frenetic, and mostly fun other than the fight against multiple oppressions in two countries. Neither of us had expected to be in a long-term relationship, let alone as husbands and dad/baba. Along the way, we've learned lessons to sustain ourselves as a couple and research has helped. Dr. John Gottman's couples counseling and divorce prediction work helped us as a couple, and we have minimized stonewalling, defensiveness, and criticism, and have never shown contempt toward each other. When we've done workshops on how to affirm LGBTQ couples, we share Gottman's work on counseling couples to bid for attention, honor each other's dreams, and work toward a ratio of 6 positive comments/interactions for every negative one as essential tools for our (and others') couple success. As Kalani matured and became more independent, we had more time to socialize with other LGBTQ folks and straight friends and have relished new friends we connect with through Twitter, Facebook (Lance) and activism in LGBTQ family and queer Asian and Pacific Islander organizing in the USA and Taiwan. This was a welcome development for us as in our second decade as parents as the first decade and full-time jobs meant we barely had time for each other; friendships were at a distance.

The other evidence-based technique that has helped us has been *Myers-Briggs Type Indicator (MBTI)*. With my extroversion and Lance's introversion, we've learned to appreciate the differences even in the most stressful moments. When we met, Lance was more of the Judging type (organized, linear) and I was more of the Perceiving type (disorganized, circular). But after many years in academe, I crossed over to the Judging side, but not as much as Lance. We both share the other two characteristics—intuitive and feeling. MBTI has been a touchstone to remember in times of conflict. Another tool that we've used is that we don't go to other persons (friends or family) when conflict arises between us. We do not triangulate others and settle our concerns together. This makes for low drama because others don't get in the middle to resolve conflict. We are also good at daily communication be it over a digital device or checking in late at night. We make rituals a priority including regular meals together both at home and finding the best ethnic cheap eats/street food from varied world cuisines.

We are in love 25 years after we met. However, we have only taken a few week-long trips on our own since Kalani was born, and in the summer of 2017 we snuck off to Quebec City, Canada for the 20th anniversary of our illegal Chicago wedding. I surprised Lance with the destination for some well-deserved couple time. Everyone else in the family thought we would be traveling to a friend's place in Costa Rica but they guessed too far south. We look forward to more time and travel together now that Lance has retired and as Kalani nears college. We especially look forward to trips in 2019 to Taiwan, Canada, Scotland, England, and the Netherlands that combine Kalani's college visits with travel abroad.

At a workshop in Taiwan in 2017, an audience participant asked us to define how we handle love, and I shared the story of how we met and have maintained that early connection ever since due to shared values and worldview. Part of that was our commitment to becoming parents. That journey was even more surprising than becoming a couple due to my sister's gift in terms of surrogacy and ensuring legal protections for our family. Even with gay marriage now legal throughout the USA (for now, depending on the composition of the Supreme Court), there is much legal gray area for LGBTQ persons worldwide from housing, employment protections, immigration, health care access, and freedom from discrimination. Similarly, while Taiwan is guaranteed gay marriage in 2019 through the Supreme Court ruling, the referenda votes in November of 2018 that saw two-thirds of Taiwanese vote against it color how it may be handled by the Legislative Yuen.

With the resignation of the "moderate" Judge Kennedy from the Supreme Court of the USA and his replacement with a 5th conservative ideologue, Brett Kavanaugh, it is possible that nationwide USA gay marriage and abortion rights may be overturned in a future Supreme Court decision, which would return gay marriage to a state-by-state legal right. Too many countries and religions still condemn LGBTQ persons--a far cry from affirming us and our relationships as evidenced by an influx of $30 million (US) to fight gay marriage in Taiwan from conservative Christians with wealth and power much greater than their actual numbers in Taiwan but easily financed by conservative anti-gay forces rooted in the USA. But gay marriage alone is not enough legal protection for LGBT persons either in Taiwan, the USA or elsewhere abroad.

WE'RE HERE, WE'RE QUEER, WE'RE STILL FIGHTING FEAR

Parenting has been a joy--most of the time--and a constant learning experience. Kalani's career interest is art and design and we encourage them to attend college abroad as our commitment to international education continues. We are excited to watch the next steps in Kalani's journey as a young adult independent from our home. Our original interest in equity and social justice has shaped our parenting in unique and powerful ways. While we can't predict the future, with Lance retired, I plan to retire from Lehman College in 12 years. We have been saddened by the overt racism Lance has faced in Newtown, PA and will return to live in New Jersey once Kalani is finished with high school--in a third Middlesex County community--New

Brunswick--near the train station so I can commute to work without driving for the first time in decades and to return to a small city after many years stranded in the suburbs.

We also plan to travel to Taiwan as often as possible (especially Lance) and look forward to retiring to Taipei's Beitou neighborhood, where I hope to assist with a dog rescue/bubble tea cafe staffed by homeless LGBTQ folks, inspired by the work of Glenn Greenwald and David Miranda in Rio de Janeiro. in Taiwan we can eat fresh seafood and tropical fruit, stroll Night Markets, enjoy hot springs, eat pineapple cakes and sun cakes, explore urban and rural flora and fauna, push for left politics, and advocate for social justice issues in two countries including LGBTQ marriage equality, LGBTQ education K-12, surrogacy, comprehensive sexuality education, immigration rights, anti-racism, anti-classism, environmental justice, voting justice, grassroots democracy, and anti-violence/anti-war issues for future generations.

Our dual-national gay marriage has united us, created our teen, and strengthened our family of origin and our family of choice in Taiwan and the USA bridging an 8,000-mile distance demonstrating our love despite legal, political, and religious constraints, hate, and dis-information that embolden us to fight for equity against the fear, ignorance, corporate greed, conservative politicians, and religionism that drive multiple oppressions.

Appendices

Sacred Commitment Ceremony invitation:

Chen Tzyy-Liang (Lance),

son of Hsiao Bi-Lan & Chen Mu-Cheng

of Taichung, Taiwan, R.O.C.,

and

Stuart Farquharson Hayes,

son of Lois F. Hayes & Charles M. Hayes

of New Lenox, Illinois, U.S.A.,

request the honor of your affirming presence

at our sacred commitment ceremony

Saturday, the twenty-eighth of June

Nineteen hundred and ninety-seven

at two o'clock in the afternoon

Second Unitarian Church

656 W. Barry Street

Chicago, Illinois

dim sum reception celebration immediately following

R.S.V.P.

The response card:

Dear Tzyy-Liang (Lance) and Stuart:

_____   Yes. It is wonderful to affirm two men celebrating their wedding because love is sacred and it's fun to make conservative politicians squirm, so <u>see you there.</u>

_____   Yes. Since Lance and Stuart's search for an interracially accurate same-gender cake topper was fruitless, curiosity has me/us overflowing to see what lands on top of the cake instead, so <u>see you there.</u>

_____   No, I can't attend. I would love to be at the fashion event of the century, but not being a member of the fashion police, it's impossible to decide what to wear.

_____   No, I can't attend. I'm liberal--but not <u>that</u> liberal.

_____   Other. Fill in the blank:_____.

Love,

_____

Please respond by regular mail or by e-mail to lansatha1@aol.com on or before

June 14, 1997

Order of Ceremony

Sacred commitment ceremony of

Chen Tzyy-Liang (Lance) & Stuart Farquharson Hayes

Saturday, June 28, 1997, 2 p.m.

second unitarian church

Chicago, Illinois

celebrant:

roger jones

music:

Adolfo Santos, piano

Rev. Lynn Ungar

guardian angels:

Jim Coursey

Rahni Michael flowers

Alison Hayes

I Li Hsiao

Jerry Hsieh

Shu Min Lin

readers:

Mary Smith Arnold

Victoria Codispoti

Hsin-i Chang

translator:

Hsin-i Chang

order of ceremony

gathering music: Scottish bagpipes

processional

lighting of the unity candle

opening remarks

responsive words of affirmation

sacred readings

meditative moment

blessings of Chen & Hayes families

love song: "and so much more"

homily

intentions

vows of sacred commitment

exchange of rings

cups of bitterness and sweetness

pronouncement and kiss

unison singing: "love will guide us"

benediction

recessional: traditional Chinese music

B. Gay Wedding & 15-year Renewal of Vows Order of Ceremony (NY, NY)

The Gay Marriage and 15-Year Renewal of Vows

of Dr. Lance and Dr. Stuart Chen-Hayes

4:00 p.m. Saturday, September 3, 2011

Friends Meetinghouse

Rutherford Street, East Village

New York City, New York

Order of Ceremony

1. **"Somewhere Over the Rainbow"**
   by E. Y. Harburg & Harold Arlen; sung by Lance, Stuart, and Kalani
2. **Welcome and the Meaning of Today's Ceremony**
   Rev. Raymond Rodriguez
3. **Reading: "I Like You"**
   by Sandol Stoddard Warburg
   Read by Lance and Stuart
4. **"Everything Possible"**
   Written by Fred Small; sung by Lance, Stuart, and Kalani
5. **The Keeper of Our Hearts**
   Kalani shares his fathers' love with a big heart and dark chocolate.
6. **Renewal of Vows (Mandarin & English)**
7. **The Gay Marriage Pronouncement**
   Rev. Raymond Rodriguez
8. **The Kiss**
9. **Presenting the Husbands Chen-Hayes!**

C. #FIRSTGAYTEENDAY Order of Ceremony and 30 Ritual Messages (Asbury Park, NJ)

#FIRSTTEENGAYDAY Ritual Order of Ceremony and 30 Messages for Kalani

Opening
Ritual
Messages
Closing of Ritual
Dessert (Broadway Musical & Gay Pride Rainbow Donuts)
Music, Schmoozing

RITUAL MESSAGES FOR KALANI:

1. Richard Koob, Kehena Beach, Hawai'i; Kalani Honua Retreat Co-founder (with dance and life partner Earnest Morgan); Richard helped organize the first NYC gay pride parade as a Gay Liberation Front member. Richard summed up the spirit of Kalani in his memoir "Lava Love":

"Kalani's vision is to model thriving global community in a context of extended family 'ohana aloha love, home-based in nature, cultural diversity, and abundant healthful food – thereby giving people opportunities to discover and become who they are, each his/her best. Kalani, just like life, is all about change, change, change, to ensure and further the same within you, within us. We're off being the wizards the wonderful wizards that are us!"

2. Chun Chen, Taipei, Taiwan, Kalani's Liu Buo/Uncle #6, on behalf of the Chen-Huang family:

送給親愛的愷樂 (Lance reads English translation):

上聯：兼愛無私心為愷

下聯：憂事進取行為樂

橫批：陳揚四海

註釋

1.以姓名為本，以具中國傳統的對聯，送給邁入青少年的愷樂。

2.莊子 天道，「中心物愷，兼愛無私」。愷，和樂、和善之意，亦可引申為愛。上聯主要勉其為人之道。

3. 說苑，「先憂事者後樂」，以此警惕行事應以先憂後樂之理，卻又不忘積極進取之心。下聯主要勉其處事之理。

4. 陳揚，彰顯之意；四海，四方之意。書經，「四海會同，六府孔修」，意旨四方各處皆為治理。上聯與下聯之為人處事、內外兼修之後，橫批是為對其祝賀及期許之意。

Chinese couplet is for celebration or special occasions. On your birthday, Liu Buo created this couplet based on your Chinese name Chen-Hai Kai-Le to celebrate your becoming a teenager.

The first couplet is to interpret KAI. Kai means harmony and happiness. Happiness comes from selflessly loving others. This is an outward contribution for others.

The second couplet is to interpret LE. Le also means happiness and enjoyment. Joy can come from being proactive to achieve your goals. This is an inward cultivation for yourself.

The horizontal scroll is to interpret CHEN-HAI. It is to wish you that your love and deeds will shine on all "four corners" -- spreading everywhere.

3. **Larry Dembrun,** Asbury Park, NJ, Manager, The Asbury Hotel

Welcome everyone and congratulations to Kalani! First, I would like to mention that I am incredibly honored that I was asked to speak here today. When the hotel was approached several months back inquiring about the date I told Connor we need to be a part of this special day! I am going to tell everyone a quick story about my journey as a child who always knew that I was special in my own way. The reason that I say that is because I always remember hearing my mom tell people that they needed to live an authentic life and be who they are, and the world would love them. That statement always stayed in the back of my mind as I navigated through my early years while I was growing up in the South. So, when I started realizing that I was not like my male cousins who always talked about girls and had posters of people like Claudia Schiffer and other early 90s models, I knew at that point my authenticity was that I was gay and I was committing to both myself and my family that I was going to live by that statement. So, I sat my parents down on May14th, 1995, a week after my 14th birthday, on

Mother's Day, and I told them that I was about to tell them something about me but after I did, I still wanted both to love me the same way that always did. And my mother looked at me and said I will always love you know matter what! And I looked up at them, and I said those three words that in a second changes so many people's lives...I Am Gay.

I remember looking at my parents, and they had tears coming down their faces, and I remember my mom saying just be you and we will always stand by you and love you. I remember asking why are you crying and she said because you are now able to be happy and not live with that weight of fear on your shoulders. So after that, I was free and authentic and was living my 14-year-old life the way I wanted to. So while in high school I was involved in every club including Drama club, horticultural club, and even was the announcer for the volleyball team. That is where I fell in high-school love with the student manager. He was a sophomore like me and we just hit it off. We both liked Cher and fell in love with Cindy Lauper and just hung out all through high school. Our friends and family accepted our relationship. So as our senior year approached, we wanted to attend our prom as a couple but were unsure how that would go so we both spoke with our parents about our thoughts and they fully supported us and said you are who you are and love who you do! So if this is what you want, then we will make sure that no one stands in your way. And as predicted some people did not understand and did not want us to attend, but our parents stood by their word and made it happen--so, in the end, we went to prom together, and my classmates and teachers even voted me PROM KING. I would say that night is one of the best nights of my life, and I sincerely hope that you, Kalani, will be able to have a great journey like I had. I honestly think that being able to be authentic and love whom I wanted to early on in my life made me who I am today. I wake up every morning living my authenticity, and I know that is why I am who I am today. Again, let's toast Kalani and his dads for his authenticity and the great journey that he has had so far.

4. Andrew Ryan, Taipei, Taiwan, TV/radio personality and family friend

Dear Kalani,

In the very short time that I have known you, I've discovered that you are not only bright, talented and kind-hearted, you also long to make a difference in our world. Your bicultural background and connection to the LGBTQ community offer you a valuable perspective that few have, and that can fuel your future pursuits. I want to give you the blindfold which I have used in our television program (and which you used that day I came to visit). It has offered me an "eye-opening" look at my co-host Hsin-ting's world, and has made me LISTEN more intently to the sounds and people of our world. Use this empathic device as a reminder to first observe, before acting and speaking. With love and light, I wish you the happiest of birthdays, and many years of growth to come.

Andrew

5. Daniel Gramkee, Bucks County, PA photographer, & husband Dr. Scott Kleinbart:

Kalani,

You have many reasons to celebrate. The immeasurable love of your parents and from those present in person today and present in spirit are evidence of why today is so special. Your amazing sense of self is also high on the list of reasons to celebrate not only as we gather today, but each day. Your sense of self is one that many of us had at your age but, even though we were surrounded by love, may not have been able to express it as openly and confidently at this same point in our own lives. So please share your gift; always encourage others to celebrate themselves, as you celebrate who you are every day and at every age.

- Daniel Gramkee & Dr. Scott Kleinbart

6. **Alex To,** Stockton, NJ, family friend

Dear Kalani,

Being gay and being biracial, you will find out that bigots are more likely to notice your skin color and ethnicity than your sexual orientation. We as a society have made great strides for LGBT causes, but there is less progress in combating racism. If anything, racism is on the rise. I've found in my life that the important thing is not to think as a victim. Here is a personal anecdote. When I was 13, I left China and landed in Hong Kong as a refugee. I went to a private high school where many of my classmates were chauffeured in their families' Rolls Royce to school, while I took an hour long bus ride each way every day. At that time, Hongkongers were extremely prejudiced against mainland Chinese. My situation was analogous to a Mexican undocumented boy who went to Beverly Hills High. But I was determined not to feel like a victim. I made friends one at a time, overcoming their preconceived prejudices. When I graduated from High School, not only was I the valedictorian, I was also among the most popular kids in the school. Don't fall for the fortress mentality. Be a happy teenager.

Best wishes, Alex To

7. **Pete Gialloretto** & sons **Jack & James Gialloretto-Cavanaugh,** Robbinsville, NJ, family friends

TO KALANI

We would like to share our family motto with you. Whether it's before a soccer game, or on an opening night, or the start of a new day, we say the following words to each other:

BE BOLD.

BE BRAVE.

BE BRILLIANT.

Keep this in your mind, heart and soul, and you'll be able to achieve anything.

FROM Pete Gialloretto and Jack & James Gialloretto-Cavanaugh

8. **Victoria Quinn,** Kell, IL, family friend

"Kalani... Wow! I knew your dad when he was still single! I can't believe you chose Stuart and Lance to be your parents! But why should I be surprised? Congratulations on your coming of age! Life has so much to reveal to you! Remember this.... Love is all there is and there are no coincidences in life! If I can ever be there for you, know that I am! All my love, ... Victoria."

9. Angie Acain & Susan Eisenberg, Queens, NY, family friends

Happy birthday Kalani! I can't believe it's been 13 years since you first appeared on the cover of *Gay Parent Magazine* as a baby. I'm enjoying hearing about your life from your dads and look forward to hearing more. Have a wonderful 13th birthday and remember never to rush through life, take your time, and enjoy every moment.

-Angie, Susan and Jiana

10. **Lillian Chen-Byerly,** Northfield, IL, family friend

Dear Kalani:

In the thirteen short years since you've been born there have been incredible changes in not only you but in the world around us. I remember vividly your parents before you were born when they lived in Chicago where your Baba worked for an agency with a dear friend. During those days, few Asians let alone Taiwanese men were in the occupational therapy and physical therapy professions. We met at an end of the year holiday party where I actively pursued your Baba for our Taiwanese-Chinese identity connection. As we got to know each other, I was fortunate to be included in your parents' parties and celebrations, in which only a few straight people were in attendance at the time. Yet, being an older straight ally and woman, I was always respected and included. I could see the advocacy and confidence of your parents always supporting others and educating the public. I would bring my young three kids who, like you, were half Asian/Chinese and half White/English, to whatever gatherings your parents held for all ages. Often, they were the only kids, but they learned about ethnic/racial and sexual orientation diversity and how to be LGBT allies. As my mixed-race kids grew, they were influenced and always enjoyed the advice they were given by your parents who innately modeled and forged new trails that allow you now to be the person you are without fear of being alienated by others. I remember your birth and am always so proud of how you have been nurtured and supported by your great parents. May today be one where you continue to learn and grow with the knowledge we all support whatever you do. We will always be here for you and I hope you will feel the love from all of us today and always!

Hugs and love!

Auntie Lillian and family

11. I-Li Hsiao, Oak Park, IL, family friend

Kalani, it's great to hear about your many adventures with your family from your baba and daddy. It's awesome to see a young queer biracial person who has a strong sense of social justice!

I wish you a great future as you embark on the journey. I encourage you to live what you preach, live and act in accord with your beliefs. Invest in a community that will support you. Your baba and daddy are a great source of love, wisdom and comfort. At the same time, it's important to carve out your own world. Remember the importance of both community and individual strength. Pursue your passion, never give up.

I Li Hsiao

PS. I-Li made paper art of his paragraph for you to remember the day by, Kalani.

12. **Rahni Flowers and Darryl Wells,** Chicago, IL and Costa Rica, family friends

A poem in honor of Kalani Chen-Hayes's 13th birthday:

Day of the Butterfly

Through the eyes of loving hands and words of giving hearts your childhood was formed

Those of two spirits dreamed of you, given reality of her flesh and blood

Here you are, coming of age, maturity half a decade away

What will you say, who will you be?

Feel, like one who is pure of heart

Hands true of deed

Give song to those without tongues

They who are red as the terracotta pottery made by the first mothers of this land

Sing with those golden as the bright morning star

Walk with those Black as the soil that brings forth life

Hear people who cross the sky on the bridge of a rainbow

Be of peace

Be of love

Be of one with the Earth

Open your wings and fly

-Rahni Michael Flowers and Daryl Wells

13. **Leigh Harbin,** NY, NY, family friend

Kalani, my favorite memory of you is actually the night we all played euchre together. I played euchre with Stuart many years before, so the moment merged the fun of the present with the fun of the past. But this is a celebration of what's to come, and I understand I'm supposed to offer words of wisdom for the future. This is scary. So I will revert to my own heritage and begin with an Irish toast that doubles nicely as philosophy of life:

May those who love us love us

And those who don't love us

May God { or Goddess} turn their hearts

And if he (or she or other or both) doesn't turn their hearts,

May he (or she or other or both) turn their ankles,

So we'll know them by their limping.

That pretty much covers it, but I will add: Kalani, you are already wise, full of talent, love, and magic. So just be yourself and trust yourself. Know that who you are today and who you are tomorrow won't be exactly the same, and that is fine, maybe better than fine. Love yourself and love whoever you want to love. Have yourself an amazing life!

14. **Mary Lou Ramsey & Mary Swigonski**, Flemington, NJ and Provincetown, MA, family friends

Dear Kalani,

We wish you the very happiest of birthdays!

May you walk with confidence on your path of becoming the very best of who you may be.

May your days on this planet be many.

May your loves in this lifetime be true.

May you walk in grace and live each day blessed with the fullness of

beauty and strength,

power and compassion,

honor and humility,

mirth and reverence.

With love and hope,

MaryLou & Mary

15. **Cynthia Walley**, Queens, NY, family friend

Kalani:

My family and I are here to congratulate you on living your truth. Although you do not know us well, know that we support who you are. I often hear about you from your dad, Stuart. As he speaks about your achievements, I find myself being honored that he has shared this information with me. For instance, I was moved that he told me you had come out. As I reflect upon that moment, I am in awe of the strength and resolve that you demonstrate. For some youths, coming out is not always an easy process, to be yourself in a world that is constantly trying to make you something else is the greatest accomplishment. Being here today surrounded by friends and family, I know you are in good hands with the abundance of love and support to be yourself, not the perception of what others think you should be.

16. **Melissa Ockerman,** Chicago, family friend

Kalani, my dear euchre protege--

On this very special & proud day,

I wish for you love, integrity & courage too--

Because you must be brave to do what you do--

We all believe you will change the world by who you are--

Indeed, your talents & natural ambition will take you far!

Live curiously and with compassion--

and, of course, with finesse, pizazz & high fashion! ;)

Come to Chicago often & we will be so glad,

when we take back the euchre championship from your dads!

With much love & affection, sugar and confection!

Be well-

xoxo,

Mel

17. **Trish Hatch**, San Diego, CA, Professor, creator of first LGBTQ conference for school counselors and educators, and family friend

Dear Kalani,

Happy coming of age birthday!

I remember back to when I was your age and how (for me) those years were fun and exciting, but also challenging and awkward. As the only daughter surrounded by four brothers I didn't always feel like I fit in. I recall times when I wasn't sure how to act or what to do. Although I always felt very loved by my family, I didn't risk sharing my challenging feelings with my parents. I was afraid to tell them that I was being picked on at school and that I didn't know what to do about it. I didn't want to hurt them or let them down. Not asking for help impacted my confidence for a very long time.

I recently shared this memory with my parents (who are 87 and 84). They told me they wished I had shared more with them at the time so that they could have provided me empathy, support and wisdom about how to manage those awkward moments.

Kalani, you are so fortunate to have two amazing dads who are "at the ready" to listen and assist you at any time. They have created your life as a giant "safe place" for YOU to be YOU, sharing ALL of whom you are.

My hope for you on this special birthday is that you will always remember the open door, their great gift of trust, and that (even with your embarrassing moments), you'll remember your dads will always be ready to empathize, listen and provide their wisdom. Adolescence will bring its share of joys, challenges, discomforts and opportunities for growth.

The lesson from me for you today is to remember that you never have to face life's challenges alone. My hope for your is to stay connected to your dads (even when you may not agree with them). Trust your dads. Risk sharing with your dads. Open and reopen the greatest gift you have - the gift of their undying commitment to you and use it (over and over) as it is never ending.

Happy birthday Kalani,

Trish Hatch :)

18. **Sharon (Shuchu) Chao**, Taichung, Taiwan, Professor and family friend

恭喜你 長大了！

第一次在台灣的彰化見面、當時你大約才2歲左右，也是我第一次認識你的爸爸們，你們一家人到我的系上來～彰化師範大學輔導與諮商學系，開啟我的學生們對於親密關係很不同的觀點：爸爸彼此之間的愛，相互的支持，以及對你的關注，都讓我們學習到不管家庭的組成「看起來」如何，最重要的仍是彼此之間相互關心與支持的心意！而你靈巧聰慧的在我們遊戲室獨自的玩耍了兩小時，對我的學生們也是個很特別的經驗！

再一次在彰師見面（2011），你長大了，害羞的你卻有著靈活的雙眼觀察著大人的世界！去年見面時，我更看到身體以及思想都有著自己意識的愷樂!!去年你們再次回到台灣，爸爸們跟台灣的學生以及關心同志運動與福祉的朋友們有很多對話，雖然我沒能在現場，但許多人都在我回來後跟我說：很高興認識Stuart、子良老師，更高興看到你～一位安靜卻堅定的年輕人！或許那次你沒能說很多你的經驗，然而你現身在那裡已經帶來了很大的影響！很高興你將有一個屬於自己的Party，希望這個Birthday Party不僅是個長大的序曲，也將帶來更多豐富迷人的樂章，更希望你多彩的成長故事可以給更多的同志或LGBTQIA朋友們支持的力量！

Congratulations on your growing up!

I remember the first time I met you in 2005, you were about 2 years old. That was also the first time I met your dads. Your whole family came to my department, the Department of Guidance and Counseling of National Changhua University of Education, to give us a presentation. Your dads' love and support for each other and for you opened my students' eyes to see that regardless of what the family is made of, it's love that makes a family. Though you were not at the presentation that day and you stayed at the play therapy room, your ability to engage in activities calmly and inquisitively also impressed those students who stayed with you.

The next time I met you in 2011, you had grown up quite a bit. Though you seemed shy, you impressed me with your observant eyes that seem to be taking in the adult world around you. Last year when I saw you again, your self-awareness of your body and mind was so evident. Though I did not attend the workshops you all presented last year for many students and LGBTQIA folks in Taiwan, many of them have shared with me how happy they were to have met the whole family, especially you, Kai-Le, a quiet yet resolute young man! Perhaps you did not get to share many of your experiences with them but your being there has made a big difference.

I'm so happy for you on this special birthday and I hope this is not only the prelude to your adulthood, but also the beginning of a piece of exuberant charming music of your life. I also hope your colorful and powerful life stories will continue to inspire many more LGBTQIA people!

19. **Laura Zaylea,** Philadelphia, PA, Interdisciplinary Media Assistant Professor, and **Jake Muñoz,** film student, Temple University

Wishes for Kalani – from Laura Zaylea & Jake Muñoz (from Building Blocks: An Interactive Conversation with LGBTQ Families)

We had the opportunity to meet Kalani – Kalani Logan Kai-Le Chen-Hayes – a few weeks ago, to sit down with him and his parents, Stuart and Lance, to hear about how their beautiful family was created. Two things that amaze us about this family are intentionality and love. Intentionality is everywhere, not just in the beautiful and unique journey of making a baby, raising a child, becoming a person... but in each detail, each syllable of Kalani's name. Love shines through when this family talks, each person expanding upon one another's sentences, inviting each other into the conversation, and most importantly – truly listening to each other. Kalani, may you always surround yourself in such loving, self-reflexive, nurturing and peaceful communities. We are inspired by your curiosity, your kindness, your bravery and your self-awareness. Your spirit shines brightly, and it is an honor to know you. Also, thank you so much for the chocolate mousse dessert you made us – it was DELICIOUS!

Happy birthday and welcome to your teenage years! You're one of the most interesting and articulate 13-year-olds we've ever met. Today is a celebration of you and the many, layered ways you claim and discover your identity and your truth. We are so grateful to have the opportunity to share this part of your journey with you. To be as open and proud as you are at such a young age is a gift. You've got the makings of a great activist and a thoughtful adult – not to mention an awesome baker – and we wish you the best!

20. **Edward Kennelly & Arturo Reyes Rodriguez,** Bronx, NY, family friends

August 9, 2016

Dear Kalani,

Happy 13th birthday! Ed and I are so happy for your big day, and we rejoice in the person you are becoming. We have known your parents know for almost 20 years, and still remember learning about your imminent arrival at a party your parents hosted, and how excited they were for you to enter the world. A world in the early part of the new millennium that was not necessarily so forward-thinking about different types of families. Your parents have taught us so much about LGBT issues, and frankly, we had not really thought about gay parenting, much less surrogacy until your parents educated us. We've learned so much over the years, and we look at you and your parents as being important in our own LGBT education. As we have watched you from afar grow up, we have been so impressed with your creativity and intelligence. We will always remember the time you came to our annual Christmas party, and sang carols at the door for the guests— the cutest guest ever to come to our door! We would still like to hear you sing "Let it Go" from one of our favorite animated movies, "Frozen," but I understand it is passé now. From your school work to your cooking skills, we always enjoy keeping up with your adventures from your parents and on Facebook. Growing up with gay parents brings special challenges, and we have been so impressed with how gracefully you and your fathers have navigated these waters, and in fact been leaders among LGBT families. You have accomplished so much already!

Now you are entering an important milestone of your 13th birthday. Cultures around the world celebrate the teenage years as a time of transition to adulthood and recognize this biological change formally in many different ways. I am especially fond of this event in my home country of Mexico, and I have helped organize many such gatherings, most notably for girls celebrating their 15th birthday. We are so excited for you to begin your transition from childhood to adulthood, and happy to learn you identify as a gay teen. This in itself will bring new challenges, but we are very confident after watching you and your parents these past 13 years, you will flourish in the new opportunities your will encounter in the next decade and beyond. What a joy it is for us to see you have so many opportunities in your life that were not available until recently in the United States and Mexico, like gay marriage. We think your future is indeed unlimited. As another of our favorite Idina Menzel songs from "Wicked" goes, "I'm through accepting limits; 'cause someone says they're so; Some things I cannot change' But till I try, I'll never know!" We wish you a joyful and productive life, full of unlimited opportunities. Unlimited, unlimited indeed!

Congratulations, and happy birthday!!

Much love,

Ed Kennelly and Arturo Reyes Rodriguez

21. **Bertrade Ngo-Ngijol Banoum,** Bronx, NY and Cameroon, family friend

My Beloved Budding Chef Kalani, As I savored your exquisite dessert treats recently, I was in awe at how fast time has flown by. It is like yesterday, that Bundle-of-Joy photograph shared by your doting parents thirteen years ago. I have shared in your mini milestones and moments of celebration including your school performances, that Mount Holyoke College magazine cover with Grandma Lois, hearty international buffets at your fabulous family homes, LGBTQ film festivals and Gay Pride Parades, NJ Gay Men's Chorus concerts and dinners, Holiday parties at Uncle Ed's, the Chen-Hayes family annual Holiday Season updates... and your yummy pastry treats. It has been pure joy sharing in your growth into a smart, fine, funny, fabulous young man coming of age with pride, self-affirmation, self-determination and many passions -- the arts, acting, advocating, baking, dancing, singing, reading, and more. With your knowledge of self and society, soar to the best of your abilities with the sky only as a limit, being your very best and doing your very best always. That is LOVE that never fails!!! BLESSED BIRTHDAY!!! -Aunt Bertrade With lots of LOVE always.

22. **You-sheng Hsu,** Taipei, Taiwan and San Diego, CA, Taiwanese gay writer/novelist/activist, first gay man married to another man (Gray Harriman) in Taiwan

人們經常為「勇敢」這一個詞下錯定義，勇敢，並不是什麼都不怕；如果有人什麼都不怕，那很可能是他從不思考事情的後果，只有一股蠻幹的氣力。
我們一生中，總會害怕一些什麼？但面對那些讓我們畏懼的事情時，如果思索那是對的事、那是該被完成的事、那是應該有人承擔的事，於是我們下決心要為此一目標，努力克服心中的害怕，去做這些事，能夠踏出這種跨越，才是真正的勇者。

Kalani:

People often mistakenly define "courage" as "not being afraid of anything." However, if someone is not afraid of anything and not considering any consequences, that's being reckless, not being courageous. In reality, we will always be afraid of something. When we face our fear, it takes true courage to consider what's right and what needs to be done, to take responsibility, to overcome our fear, and to achieve our goal. This ability to overcome fear is the real definition of courage!

23. **Jami, Brett, Emma, and Hanna Gampper,** Plainsboro, NJ, next-door neighbors

Dear Kalani,

We are so happy and honored to share some inspirational words as we celebrate your 13th Birthday and coming out ritual. We started thinking about what words of advice or anecdotes to share. Then, Lin Manuel Miranda, spoke beautiful passionate words to remember and live by that sum up what we should share with you today.

"We live through times when hate and fear seem

stronger. We rise and fall and light from dying

embers remembrance that hope and love last

forever. Love is love is love is love is love is love

is love is love, cannot be killed or swept aside...

Now fill the world with music, love and pride."

~Lin Manuel Miranda

Always be proud and true to yourself!

Love,

Jami, Brett, Emma, Hanna and Zoey

24. **Shannon Taylor,** Princeton, NJ, Kalani's middle school teacher/advisor.

Kind-hearted. If I had to use one phrase to describe you, Kalani, it would be kind-hearted. But that one phrase alone does not encompass the entirety of your being. In moments of difficulty, your quiet strength guides you. This determination is evident in all aspects of your life and serves you well. The passion with which you approach life is another great quality, one I hope you never lose. You possess the soul and experience of a much older person, but it is balanced by moments of youthful innocence. That innocence drives your curiosity, which, in turn, sparks questions. These questions lead you to interpret the world around you in your own unique way. Kalani, you have been more fortunate than most teenagers - the important people in your life have always encouraged you to listen to your own heart and mind. As you enter this next chapter of your life, your courage to do so will only grow stronger. Whatever paths you choose in life, I know you will walk them with confidence and pride.

Shannon

25. **Emma Johnson,** Hopewell, NJ, elementary/middle school classmate

My first favorite memory of Kalani was on the the way to Blairstown (camping trip for school). It was Kalani, Nina, Nina's parents and I all in the car. I remember when I packed a small bag so there could be some room for whomever needed it. Nina said she packed a small suitcase. When Kalani and Stuart started putting Kalani's things in the car with help from the Bergmans, Kalani didn't pack for three days and two nights--he packed for a month. I remember how much fun we had laughing about it for a good ten minutes. He then told me as we were about to depart that his tent was taking up most of the room. We had such a good trip up. I had fun because I got to spend the car ride with two of my good friends. I have another favorite memory and that was the first time we went to a school dance. The DJ started playing music and Kalani just started dancing. I said to my friends he is such a good dancer. I like to call him the dancing machine. I'm personally not the best at dancing but after seeing Kalani dance I learned a thing or two from him.

-Emma Johnson

26. **Nina Bergman,** Princeton, NJ, elementary/middle school classmate

Kalani has always been a lover of books. I can't remember a time when he wasn't reading the latest book in a series, or talking about the various fandoms that he was a part of. The books that I usually saw him reading were in the fantasy or dystopian genres, filled with magic, runaway teenagers, and most of all, bravery. But Kalani didn't just read about bravery; he embodied it, beginning to write his own story. That's why, on Valentine's Day of 2014, he stuck little heart-shaped valentines in the envelopes of many people at school, with the words, "I am gay." He wasn't sure how people were going to react, and there was a chance of a negative response. The action of coming out required more courage than any character he could have read about in a book had, and it was inspiring. So thank you, Kalani, for showing us how to be brave. I know you will continue to teach all of us so much more as you continue writing, writing, writing your own story.

27. **Penzi Hill,** Newtown, PA, soon-to-be high school classmate

Hey Kalani,

Happy birthday! Our parents meeting at George School Orientation was an absolutely amazing coincidence because I got to meet you! I've really enjoyed getting to know you and talking with you about everything from musicals to Minecraft. I'm really happy we became friends! You're such a cool person, with awesome taste in musical theatre! You're 13 now! You're officially on my level! My advice for you for your 13th birthday is to make it an amazing year! Every birthday is a new start and a chance to make the entire year whatever you want it to be, so why not make it memorable! If I may quote the musical *Wicked,* "everyone deserves the chance to fly." With this in mind, I hope that you soar through high school and life. Have an excellent birthday and a grand 13th year!

Your Friend,

Penzi Hill

28. **Aunt Alison Hayes,** Asheville, NC

For Kalani on his 14th 13th (of August)

Smart, funny, talented…..oh wait, I only get a paragraph? OK, I better focus on a couple of your many wonderful qualities rather than the whole list. The two things that stand out for me are your incredible powers of observation and your keen sense of justice. Whether looking at something in nature, watching a performance, or reflecting on an interaction between two people, your astute remarks always blow me away. You apply your analytical mind to generate genuine insight from the data you quietly gather. The maturity evident in what you say suggests a wisdom and depth that few attain at your age, if ever. You also have a strong sense of right and wrong. That innate sense paired with a deep-seated empathy means you care deeply about people who face injustice. With your exceptional mind and heart, I have no doubt that you will be a force for positive change in the world-- and you will do so with fun, exuberance, and style. My advice: seek out the company of those who do good by bringing out the best in the people around them. Avoid people who talk of justice but use the cover of righteousness to treat other people badly. How will you know which is which? Well, a sense of humor is often a good indicator. If a person or an organization is all angry all the time, that's not where you want to be. Find the people who know how to express joy as well as anger, who attack arguments not people, who value you as a whole person and don't try to box you in with a single label or require you to sign on to a manifesto. Let the paraphrased words of the great activist Emma Goldman be your guide: "If I can't dance, I don't want to be part of your revolution."

29. **Baba Lance Chen-Hayes,** Newtown, PA

Dear Kalani,

You've always been a gift to me since the day you were born. You were born before my 40th birthday and made my 40th birthday extra special. I thought as a parent it's my job to teach you but instead you've taught me many lessons. You've taught me to live in the moment, to be present emotionally, to listen well, to look at the world with a sense of wonder and curiosity, and to embrace life with gusto. Because of our similarity in personality, I need to look even deeper into myself to learn to love and accept myself as I learn to be a better parent for you.

I've told you many of my stories so I'm not going to retell these stories today. I do want to tell you again and again how proud I am of you! You've become this wonderful amazing young man beyond what I've dreamed of you to be. You are kind and loving. You have a great sense of justice and your critical thinking skills are beyond your age. Your love of reading is awe-inspiring. You are creative and artsy in so many different ways. You have a good sense of responsibility and you know what you need to do, well, most of the time.

One thing I want you to never forget is that I love you always. Be strong and resilient! Be proud of who you are. Be proud of your family and the uniqueness of your upbringing! I know you will do great things in your life and you will make (and already have made) a difference in other people's lives!

Baba

30. **Dad Stuart Chen-Hayes,** Newtown, PA

Dear Kalani:

13 years and about nine months ago you were conceived in a very special way connecting the Chen-Hsiao and Hayes-Farquharson-Logan families forever. One thing we didn't discuss almost 14 years ago was your sexual orientation. When it emerged early on that you were gay, you sure picked the right family. It has been a wondrous and serendipitous journey to watch your life unfold. Today is your first gay teen day in a world of opportunities and challenges. My favorite images of you are your love of dance and movement including age 2 at a Native

American pow-wow where you were mesmerized by the Fancy Dancing and had to join in; your many visits to the woods and nature from picking wild raspberries to building clay and wood structures; your love of singing and "defying gravity" with musical theatre, your skill as a pianist, your voracious love of reading, your joy in creating whole new digital worlds in Minecraft; your skill at educating hundreds of adults and kids in the USA and Taiwan on LGBTQ kids, books, and families; and your culinary presence as a rising force in the baking world. My favorite image was your speaking truth to power during your 8th grade graduation ceremony speech using your humor, sense of fairness, and courage to challenge school administrators who refused to acknowledge student's voices, bullying, or change racist and heterosexist school policies. Your courage to be all of whom you are and speak your truth is inspiring. I envision decades more of you dancing off into the sunset, baking tools in hand, making the world a better place. This loving community of friends and family are by your side in all your adventures. *Wo ai ni, Wo men ai ni* (I love you, we all love you).

-Dad Stuart